6/01

COLLECTING

BASEBALL CARDS

21st CENTURY EDITION

BY THOMAS S. OWE

D1401589

1947 ROOKIE OF THE YEAR

ERNIE LOMBARDI

THE MILLBROOK PRESS   BROOKFIELD, CONNECTICUT

To Diana Star Helmer

The author wishes to thank the following card companies for their assistance and cooperation in
providing illustrative materials for the interior and cover of this book:

Fleer Trading Cards; Los Angeles Dodgers; Pacific Trading Cards, Inc.; Philadelphia Athletics Historical Society;
Playoff Corporation; Robert Edward Auctions; Sports Stars Publishing Company; T.S. O'Connell & Son Ink;
Team Best Corporation; The Topps Company; Tot Holmes Publishing; The Upper Deck Company, LLC.

Library of Congress Cataloging-in-Publication Data
Owens, Thomas S., 1960-
Collecting baseball cards : 21st century edition / Thomas S. Owens.
p. cm.
Includes index.
ISBN 0-7613-1708-2 (lib. bdg.)
ISBN 0-7613-1478-4 (pbk)
1. Baseball cards—Collectors and collecting—Juvenile literature.
[1. Baseball cards—Collectors and collecting.] I. Title.

GV875.3.O84 2001
796.357'0973'075—dc21   00-037998

Published by The Millbrook Press, Inc.
2 Old New Milford Road
Brookfield, Connecticut 06804
www.millbrookpress.com
Copyright © 2001 by Thomas S. Owens
Printed in Hong Kong
Library edition 1 3 5 4 2
Paperback 1 3 5 4 2

TABLE OF
CONTENTS

CHAPTER ONE

PICTURE PERFECT

For as long as there has been professional baseball, there have been baseball cards.

It all goes back to 1869, when the Cincinnati Red Stockings became baseball's first-ever professional team. That same year, some smart businessman printed a brown-toned photo of the 10-member team. The $3\frac{15}{16}$ by $2\frac{3}{8}$ inch photo could be viewed through a magnifier that looked something like a Viewmaster toy.

The card, called a "cabinet," listed team members on the back — but left space open for advertising. When merchants purchased copies of the card (75 cents a dozen, or $5 for 100) their ad was printed on the cabinet back — for example, "Peck and Snyder, Wholesale Dealers in Base Ball Players Supplies." The card could be given to customers.

Price guides estimate that a near-mint example of this card, which might be the first-ever, would be worth $20,000 today.

Like many of today's cards, the Red Stockings card was a "regional." It was only available near Cincinnati, where the printer sold to local businesses. The first cards offered nationwide appeared in packages of tobacco back in 1887. Goodwin & Co. made many brands of cigarettes, including Gypsy Queen, Old Judge, and Dogs Head. Packages and cards were smaller then. Cards measured just $1\frac{1}{2}$ by $2\frac{1}{2}$ inches, inserted in the pack beside the smokes.

But even then, people were concerned about the dangers of smoking. That's why the famous shortstop Honus Wagner, known as "the Flying Dutchman," insisted that his card be removed from the packages. The Pittsburgh

Ward was one of only 10 baseball players in the 50-card multi-sport World's Champions set found in cigarette boxes in 1887.

Pirates star supposedly thought tobacco companies were trying to trick kids into smoking.

Nearly all cards showing Wagner were destroyed to avoid his threat of legal action. Hobby historians estimate that just 50 to 100 Wagner specimens survive from this series, called "T206," issued from 1909 to 1911. In 1999 one of the rare Wagners sold at auction for $325,000.

While the "non-smoking" version of the Wagner card story is exciting, some collectors believe another tale. They say that Wagner was upset because producers of cigarette cards didn't pay players for using their names and faces on them. Wagner is considered the first player in history to insist on receiving part of the profits for being included on baseball cards.

The Honus Wagner "T206" card was issued in 1909. Less than 50 examples remain. In 1996, the card sold at auction for $640,500. A 2000 Internet auction sold a Wagner for $1,265,000. Ironically, Wagner appeared in the 1948 Leaf set (as a coach) holding a package of chewing tobacco, casting doubt on his anti-smoking beliefs.

CARD FUN FADES DURING WORLD WAR I

Card-makers experimented from the start with new product combinations, new designs, and new materials. The 1914 set catalogued as "B18" is known as the "blanket" set. These baseball cards were printed on felt and wrapped around cigarette packs. The $5\frac{1}{4}$ inch squares were sometimes sewn together to make a blanket.

But the tobacco-card craze died out in 1917, when World War I filled the thoughts of Americans young and old. Candy companies tried issuing baseball cards in paper panels during this time, with several cards on one section. These cards looked and felt different than their tobacco counterparts, with posed studio portraits glued onto thick cardboard. The biggest success came from the candy company that baseball made famous.

Pitcher Addie Joss was in the T206 series that spanned the years 1909 to 1911. Ads on card backs can be found for 16 different cigarette brands. Joss appeared on few cards. He died of meningitis at age 31.

Remember the song "Take Me Out to the Ballgame," and the line "Buy me some peanuts and Cracker Jack"? That snack company issued sets in 1914 and 1915.

The card market was quiet until the 1930s, when gum companies discovered that their chewy product would sell faster if cards were included. Goudey (pronounced GOW-dee) Gum, a Boston company, became the decade's biggest name in cards, offering sets from 1933 to 1941. But during the 1940s, cards weren't a top priority, either by companies or the public. World War II was more important than baseball or collecting baseball cards. Kids may not have recognized the faces on cards made at that time, anyway. Nearly all of baseball's top names had left the diamonds. They were overseas wearing military uniforms.

Oddly, the war threatened cards that had already been printed. Paper was scarce, and many cards were recycled for use in the war effort. Sometimes, kids chose to donate their collection. Other times, parents made the decision for them. This could have been the time when the complaint, "My parents threw out my baseball cards!" became famous.

PEACETIME CARD BATTLES

Bowman was the first major company to create and market a baseball card set nationally after World War II. Beginning in 1948, Bowman issued yearly editions of as many as

Can I borrow those legs? Unfold a 1911 Mecca Double Folder, and the switched torso changes the body image into another player.

Hassan Triple Folders featured three cards in one panel in 1912. Backs described the two players and the action photo in the middle.

In 1888, Old Judge and Gypsy Queen cigarettes issued a 50-card Champions set. Anson was one of just eight baseball subjects.

240 cards. Topps became a rival in 1951. But Topps wasn't new. It had made chewing gum since 1938 (the gum was later renamed Bazooka).

Many players appeared in sets produced by both companies. But some, like Stan Musial, agreed to Bowman exclusives. Topps and Bowman began battling to secure players for their sets alone.

The combat between Bowman and Topps brought the quality of cards to new heights. The

Only four cards among the Turkey Red Cabinets featured multi-player action.

407-card set issued by Topps in 1952 represented a new record in set size. These cards also broke ground by including statistics from 1951 and a player's career; most other cards offered only mini-biographies.

Bowman struck back in 1953 with improvements of their own. Their card size increased from 2 by $2\frac{1}{2}$ inches to $2\frac{1}{2}$ by $3\frac{3}{4}$ inches. Also, instead of featuring paintings of players, or black-and-white photographs hand-colored by an artist, Bowman's new cards contained full-color photographs and nothing else — no writing, nothing to interrupt the picture.

But the competition was too much. In 1955, Bowman issued its last set — with wood-grained borders meant to look like the cabinet of the newly popular color television sets. Topps purchased its competitor and, beginning in 1956, no longer feared other companies luring players away.

Some 33 years later, Topps issued sets under the Bowman name, in addition to its regular Topps line.

Twenty-five boxers and 100 baseball players make up the 1911 Cabinet set. Mailing in coupons found in packages of Turkey Red cigarettes was the way to get someone like Ty Cobb on these $5\frac{3}{4}$ by 8-inch cards.

A set of postcards issued in the early 1990s by Tot Holmes honored cartoonist Willard Mullin. Mullin was a sports cartoonist with the New York World-Telegram from 1934-1967, drawing thousands of serious and funny accounts of the Brooklyn Dodgers and other teams. Mullin popularized the "Bum" as the cartoon mascot for the Brooklyn team. Surprisingly, Mullin's work never appeared on a single baseball card during his career.

Copyright ©Holmes Publishing, through the courtesy of Shirley Mullin Rhodes

CARDS WITH MEATS, EATS, AND MORE

Even with only one major card publisher, the 1950s was a decade that offered collectors many choices. Red Man Chewing Tobacco issued cards with the purchase of a pouch. Detachable tabs on card bottoms could be sent in for a prize, such as a baseball cap, from the collector's favorite team.

Baseball cards were sometimes included in packs of cookies, on the tops of paper cartons of ice cream, with potato chips, in bread bags, or on the bottom of hot-dog packages. The food tie-ins were endless. You could eat your way to a bigger collection! The biggest problem was the mess. Not from the eater, but from the shared space. Many cards suffered grease stains, hotdog moisture, or other grocery store accidents.

Innocent collectors sometimes added to a card's woes. Consider the cards offered by a Cincinnati meat company. Kahn's adorned their first 1950s cards with the words, "Compliments of Kahn's Wieners — The Wiener the World Awaited." Not surprisingly, many young fans liked the Reds more than hot-dog slogans. Kids cut the bottoms off the cards. Today, those cropped cards may be worth only half the amount of the untrimmed versions.

Collecting regionally issued sets like Kahn's has always presented fans with special challenges. For example, a Braves fan from 1953 through 1955 attending games at County Stadium could see the billboard for the Johnston Cookies factory. The company offered team card sets. However, only fans who lived in Wisconsin were likely to find Johnston Cookies in their grocery stores.

INCREDIBLE SHRINKING CARDS

In 1957, Topps made huge changes. Their cards shrank from $2\frac{5}{8}$ by $3\frac{3}{4}$ inches to the now-traditional format of $2\frac{1}{2}$ by $3\frac{1}{2}$ inches. After two straight years of horizontal formats, Topps became vertical again, making their cards seem even smaller. Card backs now included complete career statistics, sometimes adding minor-league records.

Collectors remember 1981 as a milestone in hobby history. Topps, once considered the only kid on the card-making block, had been challenged in court a year earlier. Fleer also wanted to make and distribute baseball cards. Had Topps controlled the card business unfairly, making players promise not to appear on other sets?

The judges ultimately ruled against Topps in its quest to stop other companies from producing cards. However, Topps kept the right to be the only company to offer cards with "confectionery products," meaning gum or candy. Fleer and Donruss couldn't include gum in their card packs.

Ironically, that part of the legal decision became meaningless in 1991. Topps stopped including stiff slabs of pink chewing gum in packs. Why? Collectors complained about gum stains on cards when they bought packs. And Topps must have realized that few fans liked to chew its infamous creation.

These 1934 Goudey cards had biographies on backs supposedly written by Yankees star Lou Gehrig. Other cards claimed to have backs authored by National League star Chuck Klein. The Boston company made the facsimile autographs of Gehrig and Klein more prominent than the names of featured players.

In 1993, Upper Deck created an All-Time Heroes set based on the T202 Triple Folders issued more than 90 years earlier.

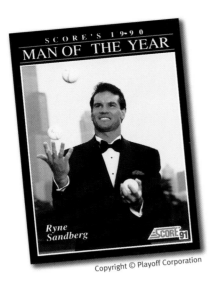

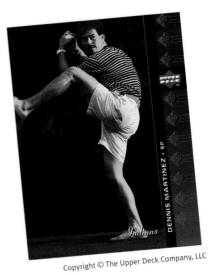

Cards of the 1990s, such as this 1991 Score, or Upper Deck's 1994 SP (Super Premium), broke a long-standing hobby tradition. Cards could show players out of uniform!

Meanwhile, more card-makers entered the fray. Score began production of baseball cards in 1988, with Upper Deck following a year later. But before the 1990s ended, Score would go out of business. Donruss, bought by Score (renamed Pinnacle), would be bought by Playoff, a football-card company. Pacific remained the decade's "new kid" in hobbyland.

Many fans were angered by the 1994 player's strike, when highly paid players demanded more money and refused to play until they got it. Part of the 1994 season was canceled, along with the World Series. Fans felt that players didn't care about fans. Why should fans care about players?

Card companies changed. Quantities lessened. As time went by, however, hobby sales became steadier as fans forgave the game. True fans always forgive the game. They know that players come and players go, but baseball is forever.

One of Upper Deck's innovations was using multiple exposures of an action shot to create an animated effect.

Action Packed never got a license from Major League Baseball to print cards of current major leaguers. Their 1992 All-Star Gallery featured 84 retired stars, portrayed in photos with a raised, three-dimensional surface. A 1995 Scouting Report set featured 72 minor leaguers.

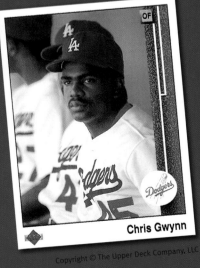

Upper Deck debuted in 1989. Its first set surprised collectors with photos larger than on other companies' sets.

In baseball, starting pitchers are judged by their condition. After five innings or more, they may not look as sharp as they once did.

The same holds true for baseball cards. When it comes to determining how much money a card is worth, condition matters more than the name and face on the card front. A Roberto Alomar card in poor condition shouldn't bring any more money, or interest, than a shredded card of any no-name baseball drifter.

All cards get graded, no matter how new or old they are, no matter how famous the faces. Card conditions with their common abbreviations include:

MINT (MT)

A mint card has no problems, large or small. In fact, the word "mint" means new, or just made. A mint card has four sharp corners, a well-centered picture with borders equal on all sides, and all edges intact. The card still has a shine, with no scratches from handling or fading from too much light. Likewise, a mint card is free from all printing problems, such as ink blobs or out-of-focus images.

To some hobby minds, "mint" means in perfect, *original* condition. Cards printed in sheets or on cereal boxes should not be cut out if you want the cards "mint."

Copyright © Playoff Corporation

A Donruss Pop-Up would be found in each three-card pack of 1988 All-Star cards. While these cards were meant to create three-dimensional figures, no punched-out card would be considered a mint specimen.

NEAR MINT (NRMT)

In school terms, this would be an "A-" instead of an "A+." This card would have one minor flaw, easier to spot. To fall to NRMT, a card might have one corner that has lost most of its point, or all corners might have a bit of wear. The image on the card front might be slightly off-center for one border. Printing quality might be less than perfect. One or both card sides might have been very slightly scraped. However, the card surfaces are still bright, shiny, and smooth.

EXCELLENT (EX)

This uncreased card will have corners that are mostly sharp but not perfect. Off-center borders may appear, along with a slight scuff or dullness from rubbing against other cards.

VERY GOOD (VG)

Sharp corners disappear from VG cards. Minor creases followed by gum stains or package damage are common problems. But no tape damage, huge creases, or ink damage will be seen.

GOOD (G), FAIR (F), POOR (P)

The grades start getting scarier here. G, F, and P hobby grades might match a "C-," "D," and "F" in class. The grade depends on how injured the card looks. These cards have different degrees of major damage. Creases large and small may be found, and all four corners may have varying kinds of wear. Card fronts are scuffed, with little gloss remaining. Some even have handwriting from the card's former owner! In the old days of the hobby — before "traded" or "update" sets were produced — young fans would edit their own cards. They would grab a ballpoint pen, scribble out the player's former team, and note his new club.

Early collectors didn't know any better. And those early days of card collecting had other problems too. Before specially designed cardboard storage boxes were available, younger, cash-strapped collectors would let cards bounce about loosely in shoeboxes. Cards might be bundled tightly with rubber bands. The rubber bands would carve grooves in the cards, or discolor cards with chemical preservatives.

Copyright © The Topps Company

To peel or not to peel? The 1996 Topps Finest cards included peelable coating, which protected the card's mint condition. However, the coating had writing on it, preventing collectors from enjoying the cards' photo fronts. But would peeling ruin a card's mint condition?

If a card in the 1950s was going somewhere, it probably traveled in a kid's hip pocket. Whoever heard of plastic protective sheets? Older collectors may remember using clothespins to fasten extra cards to bike spokes, in order to make a motorcycle sound!

Some card problems are easy to spot. But others are trickier, the difference between an "A+" and an "A."

Card injuries often begin on its corners. Once, all four corners were sharp and straight, precise right angles. Are they still? Card graders give corners five different grades, similar to A–F school grades, to note a corner's five stages of wear. Worn corners can make a card become more circular than square.

Alignment is another common woe. Most older card photos were framed by four borders. Cards sometimes lack part of one or two borders, with the photograph appearing to fall off the card front. This often happens during manufacturing, when machines cut sheets of 110 to 132 cards (depending on set size).

Some dealers might brag that cards are "straight out of the pack" or "from a factory-collated set." The message is that cards never touched by hobbyists' hands will be in better shape. But machines make mistakes too. Collectors sometimes find miscuts with half of two different cards sharing one card front!

Many older cards simply suffer from time, from incorrect storage, or from too much love. Creases are folds or tears in the card. The worst creases interrupt the photo on the card front or destroy part of the cardboard.

Hobbyists buying older cards need to be careful. Condition determines cost, and there are ways sellers can hide card problems — then charge more money.

Suppose a black-bordered card has a chip or ding. A wrongdoer could cover the mark with crayon or marker. A tougher trick to catch is the trimmed card. If a border is uneven or worn, the card is shaved with a paper cutter to make it appear straight and mint again. Only by using another card from that same set is it possible to discover that the altered card may be one millimeter smaller.

WHOSE CARDS ARE BEST?

But what if the wounded card isn't retouched? Is a card in fair-to-good condition worth the bother at all?

Many dealers would tell you that a card in poor condition is worth only 20 percent of the amount the same card in mint condition would bring. But many collectors would say the card is a worthwhile "filler." If you are trying to complete a set, a "filler" card will put you closer to your goal. After you finish the set, you can always look for nicer versions of some cards.

As the 21st century began, grading services competed to make card conditions "official." Someone would pay anywhere from $5 to $50 to send a card to a grader. The card would be returned in a sealed, protective holder ("slab"). A label attached would verify that the card was not counterfeit, while describing its condition. Coin collectors have done this for years.

Copyright © Playoff Corporation

This 1997 Pinnacle autographed card proves why collectors might think twice before asking a player for a signature.

The problem? Every service would choose a different scale, either 1 to 10, or 1 to 100. Confusion grew over which grading company knew best. Nevertheless, some collectors began paying 10 to 20 times price-guide rates for cards with the best "grades."

Try to remember that beauty is in the eye of the beholder. Your dog may be the ugliest dog in the world, but you believe no dog is better. Likewise, in the sports-card hobby, condition is in the eye of the beholder.

Would you be surprised to learn that many sellers overgrade their cards? That means: "My card is great, so pay me a lot." Of course, buyers want to undergrade, meaning: "I want that card cheaper." Before buying, it's best to see a card in person, up close, to know its true condition. To get the best viewing of a card, examine it in good light and out of its protective holder, if possible.

A card's condition determines its cost. This matters most when you are buying. So decide why you are buying this card in the first place.

Dealers will tell you that only mint cards are "collectible." But in hobby-speak, "collectible" means "worth money." If you want any card of a superstar like Hank Aaron, just so your collection includes such players, consider paying less for a lesser-condition card. Worry about great condition only if you plan to sell the card later.

Remember, "collectible" and "condition" are somebody else's rules. If your collection is just for you, you can make the rules. You can measure your success any way you want. Money is one measure of success. Fun and pride are pretty good measurements too.

> "The funny part is, I go back and look at the few cards I have left, and I see cards of coaches I have had when they were players. Guys I never heard of at the time. I picture myself 8-years-old, flipping cards. But now, I know some of these guys. Even though I didn't know who they were at the time, it's pretty funny to me. I miss the gum too, that was the second best part. The first, of course, was any New York Yankee card I got in my pack."
>
> — C.J. Nitkowski,
> former collector
> and current
> Tigers pitcher

CHAPTER THREE
INSERT MONEY HERE

In the good old days, a baseball card was just a baseball card. Sure, a few might be double-printed, making extra appearances on each printing sheet of cards. But the basic belief was that a collector had almost the same odds of pulling any particular card from any particular pack.

Then companies started developing insert cards, cards that would be randomly inserted only in *some* packs. In the early 1990s, companies called these inserts "chase" cards. The term was soon dropped, however, perhaps because the word made collectors think of a "wild goose chase."

In fact, a highly valued card from 1933 may be the first-ever "chase" card — and it was a wild goose chase. When the Goudey company released its 1933 set, none of the card packs contained Nap Lajoie, card number 106. Some angry collectors wrote to the company and got a response: In early 1934 the card was mailed to them. Guesses

---

Beginning in 1992, Donruss offered "Diamond Kings" as random inserts. One player per team would be painted by artist Dick Perez, such as Dodger Orel Hershiser in 1993. By 1995, Diamond Kings were offered on average of just one per 10 packs.

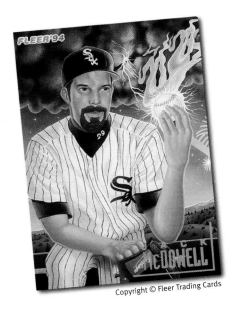

Fleer's 1994 cards averaged a Pro Visions insert in one out of every 12 packs. The nine inserts were puzzle pieces. Together, a fantasy scene would be formed.

are that less than 1,000 of the cards were made. By the year 2000, a near-mint example topped $37,000 in price guides.

Upper Deck's 1990 set deserves credit for ushering in the modern age of inserts. The nine "Baseball Heroes" cards, highlighting Reggie Jackson's career, were randomly inserted in Upper Deck's series of high-number foil packs. No one knew if a pack would have any of the special cards and, if there was an insert, which card it would be. To add to the excitement, 2,500 of the available "Heroes" cards were numbered and autographed by Jackson.

Since then, companies have kept the innovations coming. Inserts have included holograms, die-cuts, or laser-cuts (cards created in unique shapes), and cards made of leather, canvas, or other materials.

Just how rare are these inserts? Insert set names may be listed on wrappers with a notation like "1:24." Some new hobbyists wrongly believe that one of every 24 cards will be an insert. But read the fine print on the package closely. The odds actually state that you might get one insert in every 24 packs that you open.

Card companies make no promises about inserts. If your luck doesn't match the odds predicted on the wrapper, too bad. The company has no obligation to send you any cards in return.

But not all inserts are difficult to find. In fact, inserts may be the same cards you find in the basic set — with just a small change or twist. Maybe the insert card of Stevie Shortstop looks like his regular card, except the border is gold. Or his insert card features a reproduction of his autograph. "Toppsgold" and the Upper Deck "silver and gold signatures" are common examples of such variations. This kind of insert is called a "parallel card."

The extreme for a parallel card is the "refractor." Topps promoted this idea in its "Finest" and "Bowman's Best" sets. Refractor cards seem identical to their regular set counterparts. However, tilt them in the light, and they "refract" a rainbow of colors. Because the cards were hard to identify without seeing them sparkle, the company started including an "R-" prefix in front of each card number, to distinguish a refractor.

One of the strangest refractor cards was the "Mirror Black," found in some packs of the 1997 Pinnacle Certified set. Card backs were normal, with a small player photo and stats. The front of the card had the player's name but no photo: It reflected back the viewer's face. After sets were already in stores, Pinnacle announced that some packs contained these cards. Hobbyists called it a "stealth" insert, a secret, unannounced addition to packs.

Years later, after the company was out of business, a former employee told a hobby magazine that the cards were mistakes made at the printing plant. Perhaps five or less were made of each player. Only when collectors wrote to the company did Pinnacle discover this error was issued. The best idea was to tell hobbyists, "Surprise!"

Copyright © Playoff Corporation

Odds were that only one in nine 1994 Studio packs would contain a Heritage Collection card. Wearing vintage uniforms, players were posed in front of ballpark scenes from a certain year.

HERE! HAVE ANOTHER

Collectors never know when they'll encounter such happy accidents. When Donruss accidentally failed to include "Significant Signatures" autographed inserts of

Sandy Koufax in its 1988 Signatures packs, the company made an unusual promise. Anyone who got a card number 18, a signed Billy Williams, could mail it back to the company. In return, Donruss would send back the Williams card *and* a signed Koufax.

This mail-in technique has been used by other companies on purpose. A company can't fold up an 8-by-10 autographed photo or other huge bonus in a pack of cards. Instead, pack buyers may find a "redemption card" that reads, "You won! Mail this in to get . . ." Collectors, however, must read carefully and act quickly. Such offers usually have expiration dates.

The worst expiration date is one that's unannounced. Collectors who tried to redeem their winning insert cards from Scoreboard in 1999 got a huge shock. Instead of the autographed memorabilia promised on the card, all the hobbyists received was news that the company had declared bankruptcy. The out-of-business company left many collectors empty-handed and with bitter memories.

Upper Deck had trouble with its 1999 inserts too. In earlier inserts, the company had featured pieces of uniforms from active players attached to cards. The stunt had gone over well. Later, the company bought a bat used by Babe Ruth for $23,000 at auction. Upper Deck created 50 different inserts, each containing a shaving off the Bambino's club.

Sportswriters were horrified. How could Upper Deck destroy a precious piece of baseball history?

Upper Deck quickly explained that the bat they'd purchased had a cracked handle, which could have led to it splintering on its own. Furthermore, the bat hadn't

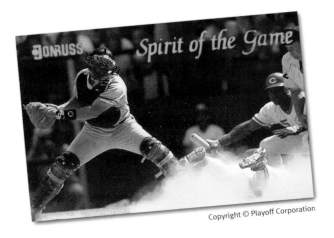

Foil and jumbo packs of 1993 Donruss contained these random Spirit of the Game inserts. Despite showing runner Bip Roberts, catcher Damon Berryhill, and batter Glenn Braggs, cards like this that include multiple players aren't always worth more.

BOBBY ADAMS
third base CINCINNATI REDLEGS

Copyright © The Topps Company

When Topps Archives reproduced its 1954 set in 1994, a "parallel" set was offered. Each 10-card pack contained one "Gold" card, with facsimile autograph and team logo set off in gold foil.

been used for any record-breaking hits. And the company wasn't destroying the last Ruth bat on Earth: 100 different Ruth bats were still on the market.

Upper Deck continued to have bad luck with its 1999 inserts. Its 1999 Century Legends packs contained one, and only one, "Legendary Cuts" insert — an actual autograph of Roy Campanella. The lucky owner of the card told *Beckett Baseball Card Monthly Magazine* that, as soon as he got it, he sold it. "It's the ugliest card I ever owned," the seller said. He explained that the signature (signed before Campanella's paralyzing car accident in 1958) was on thin paper, possibly from an autograph book. Another autograph from the other side of the paper was bleeding through, ruining the look of Campy's penmanship.

HOW RARE IS RARE?

The most common problem is one that's been around from the beginning of inserts: Companies still stall in telling production numbers.

That's why more and more current inserts feature separate, sequential numbering. If only 500 of a certain card are being produced, the card might read "250 of 500." This does not mean that 500 different players are featured in that set of inserts. Instead, the number indicates that there are 500 cards like yours, and yours was made in the middle of the print run.

But are these labels enough? HBO television's *Real Sports* news program asked that question in a disturbing story about insert cards in December 1999. The segment, titled "Cardboard Crack," told of a teenage boy and a lawsuit. The boy claimed he wasted more than $10,000 on packs of cards, with the failed hope of finding pricey inserts.

Pacific made 20 players into Christmas ornaments for one of 2000's most talked-about inserts.

An attorney insisted that card companies, with the consent of Major League Baseball (MLB), knowingly provide minors with gambling opportunities. The attorney compared tempting youngsters with inserts to selling lottery tickets to children. The TV reporter noted that the attorney hoped the lawsuit would gain class-action status. This would mean that thousands of other young people and their families could join the lawsuit, with everyone seeking a cash award to punish the card-makers.

Like many collectors, the boy prompting the lawsuit may have believed that the value of insert cards would rise each year, due to their limited supply. But demand plays a big part in value. Chances are that year-old inserts will be surpassed in their technological dazzle by the new crop of special cards. It's just like a movie rental store. The new releases often cost the most. Counting on a card's value increasing is, indeed, a gamble.

No matter how old or young the buyer, it's the attitude about inserts that defines if making a purchase is gambling. What is the buyer doing with the other cards in the pack? Does the insert chaser think that all cards in the pack are garbage if the big-dollar insert card doesn't magically appear?

If that's the case, collecting may be the wrong place to be. The stock market is for making money. Baseball cards are for making memories.

"If we don't do what people like, we won't get to play anymore."

That's the card-making rule of Michael Cramer, founder and Chief Executive Officer, of Pacific Trading Cards. And Cramer has a good idea of what people like. Through the years, whether working as a fisherman, card dealer, or card creator, Cramer never stopped being a collector.

Since 1990, Pacific has been headquartered in Lynnwood, Washington. The entire operation is located in one building — card designing, printing, packaging, and shipping — an uncommon feat among companies.

Cramer started his first hobby business in 1960, as an Arizona eight-year-old. "My mission was to have more cards than anyone in the world," he said. In his office, he keeps the first card he ever traded for, displayed in the frame he hand-lettered as a kid, reading "My First Baseball Card." It's a 1960 Babe Ruth, one showing lots of wear.

The Babe was just the beginning. "Even in high school, I was buying cards. I made $1,000 mowing yards one summer, and I spent it all on cards," Cramer said. "My friends would give me their cards, or I'd give them a couple of bucks for their cards" when they thought they were too old for collecting, he said. "I was one of the first guys to put ads in the paper to buy cards — and

Copyright © Pacific Trading Cards, Inc.

Only 10,000 of these inserts were produced for random inclusion in Pacific's 1993 packs. Fronts used a silver foil background.

Pacific made just 8,000 of each Home Run Leader, like Frank Thomas. These inserts were sprinkled through 1994 packs.

to sell some leftover cards. Everyone, even my parents, thought I was a little nuts."

He remembers going to one of the nation's first card conventions, in 1970.

"I drove cross-country to Detroit with a trunk full of extras to sell," he said. "But when I got there — I couldn't bear to part with them. I just wanted to show them."

Starting at age 16, Cramer worked summers with an uncle as a commercial fisherman in Alaska. After high school, he worked on fishing boats until 1979. By then, he had his card-creating plans in place.

MINOR CARDS, MAJOR SUCCESS

Cramer produced his first-ever cards in 1975. Along with a trendsetting full-color Phoenix Giants AAA set from 1976, Cramer revived a decades-old concept: The only way collectors could get all 23 premium photos in a second set was to mail in Coca-Cola bottle-cap liners.

The biggest start-up challenge should have been getting photos of minor leaguers for the cards. But Cramer shrugged. "I bought cameras and equipment" — and took the pictures himself, he said. "It may sound brash, but I just did it."

Cramer's work in minor-league team sets continued through 1987. Meanwhile, "Cramer Sports Promotions" debuted. From 1980 to 1983, Cramer released "Baseball

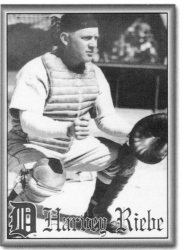

Harvey Riebe caught part-time for the Tigers in 1942 and 1947–49. He never appeared on a card during his career. In 1995, Pacific made cards of Riebe for his personal use, without charge.

Legends" card sets in four series, 30 cards per year. Featuring brown (sepia) photos of retired players, mostly Hall of Famers, the cards were offered in wax packs.

"The first wax packs were wrapped by hand and fastened with tape. So I bought two wrapping machines from a candy company," Cramer said. Computers weren't in common use yet, so Cramer's earliest cards were designed with scissors and paper. "The photos used to be held down with wax on the back" when the cards went to the printer, Cramer said. And one of Cramer's first employees was his mother, who worked in the business for 15 years.

In 1982, Cramer applied for a license from Major League Baseball, a license that would enable him to use the names and logos of all current major league teams on his cards. The League refused. Fleer and Donruss had obtained licenses a year earlier. Baseball would permit no newcomers for years to come.

Current players were off-limits. So Cramer chose to deal with past players

The 20-card All Latino All Star Team insert set was seeded in random packs of 1994 Pacific product. A total of 8,000 sets was produced.

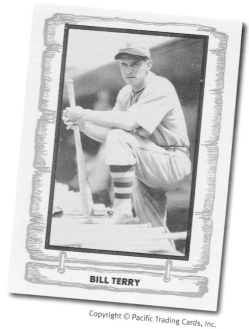

BILL TERRY

Future Pacific CEO Michael Cramer took from 1980 to 1983 to issue his first "Baseball Legends" set of 124 cards, offering one series per year. Back then, his company was called Cramer Sports Promotions.

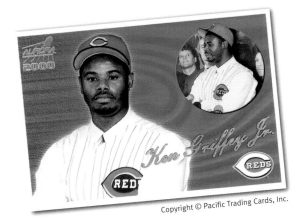

Copyright © Pacific Trading Cards, Inc.

Pacific rushed to include the newly traded "Junior"

in his new Reds uniform for the 2000 Aurora set.

directly. In 1988 a new 110-card "Baseball Legends" set debuted, featuring retired stars. Although Cramer gave both his sets the same title, the new set was full color.

"I had to learn how to do all this," Cramer said. "I didn't plan it all out. It just happened.

"I didn't talk about it. I just did it. Fishing taught me to work hard, be efficient and to not make mistakes — or you'll be dead. The boat could sink, you could land a crabpot on someone. I think if you want to learn, you can. If you're not interested," he said, "you don't learn."

After producing career highlights sets honoring Tom Seaver and Nolan Ryan in 1991 and 1992, Pacific's tide turned. Cramer asked again for an MLB license, this time to produce a card set in Spanish.

"When I proposed the Spanish set, they said, 'We've heard this before from other companies.' I said, 'Yes, but I *will do it*.'" He did, beginning in 1993.

The idea of printing cards in both English and Spanish, two sets yearly, still makes sense to Cramer. "If you go to a game, look around. Fans are Hispanic!" he said. "Twenty-five percent of players are Latino." Exporting cards to Spanish-speaking countries created a big business.

Pacific workers write the card backs in English. They send the words to a professional translator in Puerto Rico. Before work on the sets began, Cramer flew to the island to meet the translator. While confident of her skills in English and Spanish, Cramer wanted to be sure she spoke baseball — that she could translate baseball words from English to Spanish without changing the game's meaning.

"TURN AND BURN"

Pacific fields a five-person design team, which includes Cramer, public-relations director Mike Monson, and Rob Hicks, graphics manager and computer expert. (Hicks's first job with Pacific years earlier was as a truck driver.) Their mission is "turn

26

and burn" — a favorite Cramer saying describing their speed in turning an idea into a card set.

"One of the most fun things has to be the creative process," Monson said. "None of us are technically what you would call artists. We're amateurs as artists, but our ideas are second to none. We make sketches and the graphic artists downstairs turn those into fantastic die-cuts."

Most young collectors who meet Cramer and the Pacific staff at card shows talk about being card designers — not just in the future, but *now*. Unfortunately, Pacific can't use designs mailed in by hobbyists. The company has its own full-time designers.

Cramer explained other duties of the 85-plus employees at the Lynnwood headquarters. "In our media department, we have five jobs writing and editing copy (card backs). One guy's job is to read all the papers and store all the latest info. And 14 people are in the graphics department. We give them the idea, but they have to lay it out" — actually create the design on paper or on computer disk.

"There's accounting — we have four mechanics [to work on packaging machines] — there is purchasing — we have five employees in sales working with hobby shops and places like Wal-Mart and K-Mart — we have a webmaster — and a photo library. We sell photos to *Sports Illustrated* and other media. They have specific needs: They want a certain player standing, or looking right, or smiling."

Reading daily baseball updates helps Pacific to keep its cards current. "We keep informed," Cramer said. He explained how Kerry Wood was pulled from all 1999 sets, once news broke that the Cubs pitcher would be sidelined for a year due to elbow surgery.

Whatever their jobs, Pacific employees know how closely hobby scavengers are watching. Everything not used at Pacific is shredded, then recycled to keep new projects secret. One discarded card experiment might be treated as a one-of-a-kind wonder by a trash-picking collector. Cramer knows from personal experience how "garbage" can tempt collectors.

"When I was younger, a 20-something in Phoenix, I'd dive in dumpsters outside bakeshops," he said. "Hostess Cupcakes printed cards on box bottoms. That cream would go everywhere!"

CARDS OF EVERYBODY!

Pacific won the hearts of players and autograph collectors alike with its 1998 "Online" set. In this 780-card set, 750 different players were pictured. Nearly everyone in baseball had a card to autograph.

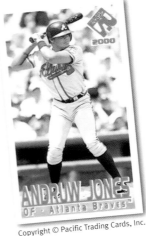

Mike Cramer's appreciation of the T206 tobacco card set shines in the 60 Private Stock 2000 inserts.

Copyright © Pacific Trading Cards, Inc.

"You make friends that way," Cramer said. So often, lesser-known "players say, 'Why pose? No one ever puts me on a card, anyway.' But they line up for *us*," Cramer said — and Pacific put them in the set. Soon players were calling Pacific, asking for extra cards to give to their parents.

Many of those players never realized that the friendly photographer in Arizona — the one who brought them 100 cards of themselves from the past set — was Cramer himself. "You can talk a lot in spring training, because the players don't have a lot to do after games," Cramer said. He has countless stories of players who act cool and quiet about getting cards, only to pop packs and play with their treasures when they think no one is watching.

The 1998 Paramount set by Pacific marked another huge victory for Cramer and company. Major League Baseball and the Major League Baseball Players Association granted the company a full license to make all-English cards. Pacific was now on the same level as Topps, Upper Deck, and Fleer — the only other companies approved to make baseball sets.

Collectors sometimes ask Cramer how Pacific decides how many cards to print of each set. The answer: Ask your local dealer.

For example, "We only made what was ordered for Prism Baseball (1999). Now dealers want it and can't get it, because they didn't order ahead of time," he said. And, after just one year, price guides valued the 150-card basic set at $100 or more.

"As an adult, and having my own cards as a player, I was at first very proud to have finally 'made it.' Every year I looked forward to see what photo they would put on the card. Some years I was pleased, other years not so. I wished that someone would have consulted me on the choice, but logistically that was impossible to ask 650 players what their favorite card was."

— Vance Law, who played from 1980 to 1991. Vern Law, Vance's father, pitched for the Pirates from 1950 to 1967.

"In the old days, people [card companies] would go back and run more [print more cards]. We don't have time. We're on to the next project. It's too expensive to print just for the heck of it," Cramer said. "In the old days, it was just ink and paper. Now it's foil, foil dyes, die-cuts — some single cards cost us over a dollar apiece to make."

Besides, he said, "If there aren't enough of a card, that's called 'collectible.'"

COMPUTERS MAKE THE DIFFERENCE

"Key" players on Cramer's creative team are found in front of computers. In the design center, curtains to the one outside window are drawn. Half the lights are off.

Top secret? Maybe. Mainly, the semidarkness helps workers see colors better, as there is less light reflecting off computer screens. Likewise, sunlight can fade paper and photos in use.

Graphics for each card takes five megabytes of computer memory. For a fancy card, up to 25 megabytes are needed. In 1999 one Pacific computer could only hold two card projects at once. The machines would soon be replaced, and the old ones donated to schools.

Editors edit 50 to 70 card backs in one day. Three people work on basic cards in a set; three work on inserts. Across the building, the walls near the printing press are insulated with extra sheets of cards from early sets, to help with the noise level. Newly printed sheets roll off the press and are machine-cut into cards. The cards are placed in small stacks that ride down a conveyor belt.

Another machine "decollates" the stacks. A pinwheel of suction-cups spins, gently lifting single cards from the stacks,

Copyright © Pacific Trading Cards, Inc.

The 450 cards in the 1997 Pacific Crown set are bilingual, with biographies in both Spanish and English.

29

A Pacific card is created, from start to finish, in the company's Lynnwood headquarters. The process begins with a player photo. Using a slide of that photo, a card is designed entirely on a computer. The computer design is transferred to film, which is used to make a printing plate. Sheets of actual cards are printed from the printing plate. After the sheets are cut, the cards are shuffled by machine into random order (decollated). Next the cards are packaged, then loaded into boxes and shipped to stores and dealers.

and, occasionally, taking one from an insert stack. This packing arrangement helps guarantee a better mix.

"We weigh each pack to make sure there is the same number of cards in each. If there is a mistake in collation, packs are opened," Cramer said.

This "turn and burn" card-maker answers to no other owner. Pacific remains in the Cramer family. The bigger companies might worry more about making mistakes and losing money. Rival companies have stockholders, many owners.

Cramer, the collector and creator, has a simpler motto. "Our cards are my favorite. I put one [of every] set away," he said. "The first set is for me. The rest are for anyone who wants one."

CHAPTER FIVE
CYBER-COLLECTING

Buying. Selling. Trading. New cards. Where? At your crosstown hobby shop, or the once-yearly card show? Try a computer!

It's happening: fast, nonstop hobby action, thanks to the Internet. Right now, in your own home, or in classrooms or libraries, computers are changing how collectors collect.

Hobbyists once had to wait for monthly magazines or the weekly *Sports Collectors Digest* to get news about new sets of baseball cards. Now these hobby media are among the last to get the news to the collecting public.

Card companies give instant reports about new cards to collectors everywhere. Just call up a company's Web site. Under "news releases" are the same stories about new sets that are sent to hobby magazines. In fact, you might see almost the same story printed in the hobby magazines several weeks later.

For instance, Upper Deck announced that some $1 million worth of game-used memorabilia would be given away month by month during the year 2000, via a mail-in sweepstakes. According to hobby magazines, entry blanks could be found in packages of cards. However, a trip to *www.upperdeck.com* revealed that there was a "no purchase necessary" choice for entering.

Internet access to teams is another way to increase your collection. The Internet can show you which teams are hobby-friendly. You can check out the upcoming schedules of pro and college teams online. Those schedules may list promotional give-aways, giving you an idea of which teams reward their fans with free cards, autograph signings, or other treats.

If the information you want isn't listed, ask for it. The Internet is an equal-opportunity medium. Your message, sent by electronic mail (E-mail), often gets instant attention. As long as your spelling and grammar are all-star quality, there is no clue that you are a kid. You are judged by your message or your request.

Some companies, however, are slow to provide a space for feedback. Others, like Topps, may be forgetful. "Home Team Advantage" is a Topps club service: For a yearly fee, members could get special cards and other buying privileges. Shockingly, willing customers couldn't get information on the *www.topps.com* Web site about the program.

Overall, hobbyists can learn a lot online, swapping information and more. Shops, dealers, and individual collectors either set up their own Web sites or try to buy, sell, and trade through forums, bulletin boards, and chat rooms. They'll leave messages about the cards they have or want. One of the most popular free Web sites for hobbyists is *www.beckett.com*, created by the famed hobby magazine.

From such a site, registered members have "profiles." It's possible to leave feedback about someone you've dealt with. Visitors may find subject lines like "Bad Trader" or "Ripped off." A common story found under such headings tells of two online collectors who agreed to trade one card each. The first collector was honest and sent his trade through the mail. But the second trader claimed the card never arrived and wouldn't send the card he promised in return. Many such stories involve inserts or rookie cards, with losses in the tens and hundreds of dollars. How do you know who is telling the truth?

After all, the remote chance exists for someone to fib. The person described may behave better, or worse, than the online "report card" indicates.

For the most part, people share their sad stories because

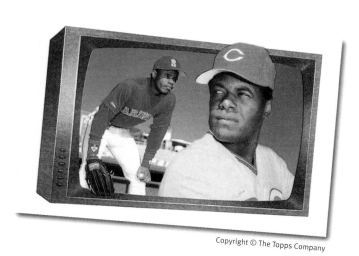

Copyright © The Topps Company

Topps revived the Bowman name in 1989 with a 484-card set. Only one card (#259, of father-and-son Griffeys) used a TV theme. The last Bowman set in 1955 had featured wood-grain borders, designed to look like a color TV set — an invention still unknown in many American homes.

they're trying to help others avoid the problems they found. Still, being more choosy about their hobby partners might have avoided their disappointments.

If you spend a couple of extra dollars to send by registered mail or United Parcel Service, you'll get a receipt after your package is delivered, written proof that it reached its destination. If you have such information, your postmaster or the Better Business Bureau (check your local telephone directory) might be able to help you get the goods that were promised in trade. Most often, the best defense is a good offense. In other words, check out the person you're dealing with before you send money or trades.

Collectors of any age should talk by telephone or mail a regular letter to get more information from new hobby people they meet on the Internet. It's a good idea to ask for names of people that your new trading partner has done business with. Then call or write those people too. Dealers who won't give you names of other people they've done hobby business with aren't worth your time. Your money and your cards are at stake.

Don't be shy about asking for opinions from teachers or other adults who've done business on the Internet before. They can help you judge if the sales pitches or trade offers sound fair and honest. We all need to be reminded sometimes of the old, wise warning: "If something sounds too good to be true, probably it is."

On the Beckett Web site, collector auctions happen daily. The most famous auction Web site

The Philadelphia Athletics Historical Society salutes the original A's, before the team moved to Kansas City in 1955 and later to Oakland. The 1998 set of 40 cards was discovered for $15 at www.philadelphiaathletics.org.

PHILADELPHIA ATHLETICS

Jimmie Foxx

INFIELD

Copyright © Philadelphia Athletics Historical Society

at the start of the 21st century was *www.ebay.com*. A rising star in the hobby field was *www.sportsauction.com*. The bad news? No one under age 18 was supposed to bid on these sites. Minors who wanted to bid were required to have an adult bid for them. Why? Pretending to bid on an item, then never paying, is more than wrong. It's against the law in many states. A bidder's word is a legal contract. Bidders who don't honor their bids might face lawsuits.

But younger collectors can still use these sites as yardsticks to measure hobby activity. Are actual selling prices above or below price-guide listings? Best of all, almost all cards sold by Internet auction are shown online. Auction Web sites are like museums. You can look and learn for free, without buying anything!

Hobbyists can learn more about basic collecting online too. Sometimes, bulletin boards or forums give a chance for visitors to "post" a comment or question for the world to consider. See if others will share their collecting experiences, such as: Did they fail to get a complete set after opening a box of packs? Did they get more inserts than the odds on the wrapper predicted? By sharing information, all collectors can spend their money more wisely and get the cards they want most.

Many public schools in many countries have their own Web sites. Find a student baseball fan who wants an "E" pen pal, and there's a chance you'll find a collector who would trade cards.

Any time the E-mail address of a team, hobby author, card-maker, or dealer is printed in an article or on a package, keep track of it. That hints that the person or company wants to know what you're thinking.

Send your questions and ideas. Don't think: "Why would someone answer me?" Instead, try asking: "Why not?" In baseball or in your hobby, you'll never get a hit if you don't take a swing first.

> "I do not even remember giving anyone permission to use my name on a card. In fact, I did not see the 1944 card until a few years ago [in the 1990s] when someone sent me the card and asked me to please sign it for them. The company never contacted me. In fact, I would like to have a couple of those cards for my own mementos. I think it's very nice to have your picture and data on a card. It is so nice to be remembered."
>
> — Don Gutteridge, card #1, 1944 Play Ball set

CHAPTER SIX

A STORE WITH MORE

Baseball teams love to play at home. A familiar field, friendly fans — it's easy to understand what the term "home field advantage" means.

Collectors can't find a better home-field advantage than the nearest hobby shop.

There's no need to order by mail or over the Internet if you have a local store that specializes in sports cards. Often called "hobby shops," these places have special shelves and cases filled with baseball cards, old and new, along with other baseball collectibles and hobby supplies.

Why should you bother with a hobby shop when a department store might save you a couple of bucks per month?

Good question. However, think of what you'll get besides cards at the hobby shop.

HOBBY-SHOP SPECIALTIES

The hobby shop might be run by hobbyists. These employees may be collectors too. If you buy a hand-sorted set of Topps, you can bet that each card was examined before it went into the box. On the other hand, if you purchase a factory-collated set offered at a department store, the store clerks may not understand your problem about one missing card or several miscut cards. They're only selling what the card-maker sent.

True, the toy store in the mall may offer the same packs a dime cheaper. But customers can't come back to that toy

The 1941 Play Ball set was made by Gum, Inc. The cards put every player's nickname in quotes, making each nickname look like an alias.

store and ask to buy the remaining four cards they need to complete a set. At the hobby shop, customers who buy a box of packs have helpers waiting. Did you get enough cards to make a set? If not, the hobby store should have a pile of common cards you can sort through, buying only cards you need.

Can you imagine telling a department-store worker that you'll only buy the best cards out of the pack? Or asking the chain-store employee to pop a couple of Bowman packs for you, because you only want a card of Vladimir Guerrero? Hobby stores do it all for you, selling the stars, the rookies, or sorted team sets — for example, all the New York Yankees cards from a certain set.

TWO DIFFERENT WORLDS

Card companies know that choosing between hobby stores and department stores confuses some collectors. That's why makers like Upper Deck produce separate packs called "hobby only" and "retail only." One kind goes to hobby stores, the other goes to chain stores. The companies will even produce different insert cards, available only in packs from one type of seller. Of course, the companies hope that collectors will buy lots of both kinds of packs, increasing profits for everyone.

Copyright © Playoff Corporation

To give collectors more chances to find more cards, some hobby shops run "bid boards." These are monthly or weekly auctions. Cards owned by the store owners, or brought in by other collectors, are displayed. Customers may see a minimum bid posted (the lowest price the owner of a card will sell it for). If there's no minimum posted, bidders can try to buy a card for as little as possible. Of course, you're

The 1993 Triple Play set by Donruss was made to be a lower-cost choice for younger collectors. Card number 11 included a childhood photo of Cubs star Mark Grace.

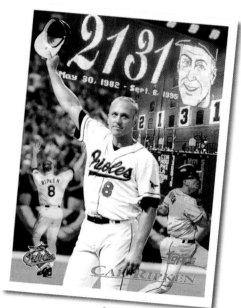

competing against other people who want the same card for the same discount price. If you set a dollar limit for yourself, and don't overspend by trying to beat other buyers, you can find some bargains.

EARLY BIRDS CAN GET BARGAINS

Here's another hobby-shop bonus: Ask your hobby store if it would "pre-order" upcoming cards you are interested in. Store owners often offer boxes of a product, such as the newest Pacific Crown Collection, at a guaranteed price. You'll pay in advance and get the box when it's shipped by a promised delivery date.

This gives the dealer money in advance to obtain a quantity of the cards. Sellers, whether small shops or huge chain stores, get better prices when they buy more. If the store pays less to get cards, it's often willing to charge you less too.

If you pass up a bulk preorder offer, you may find the dealer is selling packs you

This 1998 Topps Chrome of Jay Bell shows how the decade's cards were changing. Players had fun posing, but collectors didn't always have fun buying. The 502-card set was issued in four-card packs with suggested retail prices of $3.

could have had for $3 at a $5 rate. Perhaps the company didn't print as many cards as promised, or raised the prices it charged dealers. Maybe every collector wants a certain hot-selling rookie card out of those packs. Sometimes it's worthwhile to pay early.

A HOBBY CLASSROOM?

A hobby shop is often the place where collectors, like you, learn about new products or trends. Remember, hobbyists learn from each other. A shop owner who has been busy collating team sets may not have had a chance to read about the new rookie sensation. Owners can learn from collectors like you.

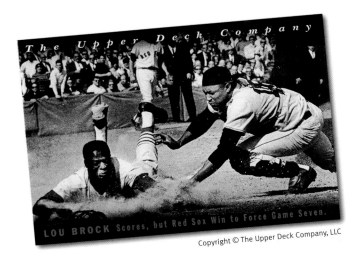

Who says all cards showing Hall of Famers are expensive? Price guides put this 1994 Upper Deck All-Time Heroes card of Lou Brock at 15 cents.

So don't complain that the hobby store doesn't get the "hot" baseball cards if you haven't told the store owner which hot cards you want! Furthermore, few stores have the time, space, or money to carry every new trading card made. Most store owners try to sell cards from all sports, to appeal to as many customers as possible.

Hobby stores offer a lot of extras. But most stores don't buy from (or swap with) customers. That's because hobby stores, like big department stores, need to make money. Workers need to be paid. New cards and products have to be bought from companies. Stores have to pay rent. Did you know that stores in some malls have to pay part of their profits to the building owners, in addition to monthly rent?

That's why a dealer probably won't pay the price-guide amount for your card. After all, when the dealer resells the card, who would pay more than price guide? And if dealers only make back the same money they pay out, there's no profit for rent and workers. The same hard facts follow dealers in trading. If you want to trade for a $10

> "Yes. I collected cards along with my dad. I still have most of them. Being featured on so many cards confirms that all the work I did as a kid paid off. Of course, if it weren't for the talent and perseverance God gave me, none of it would have been possible."
>
> — Catcher Ed Herrmann, on 25 cards from 1969 to 1979

Shawn Green card, you might have to offer $20 worth of cards in return. But remember, you're thinking of today's collection. The store owner is thinking about next month's rent.

HOBBY-SHOP SURPRISES

To reward faithful shop owners throughout the late 1990s, Fleer/Skybox would send a team of retired players to sign free autographs at top-selling stores. Hall of Famers like Bob Gibson would show up at mom-and-pop shops. Other companies have provided samples and freebies for stores to pass out and share with customers.

Maybe the best part about being in a hobby shop isn't surrounding yourself with baseball cards. The best part comes from being around so many other people who love baseball cards as much as you do. That's why some customers will stand at the counter, opening packs on the spot. Chances are that the store workers know your favorite team and player. Just like an all-star, you may get cheers when you pull out an insert or hot rookie.

Even if you aren't buying, hobby shops are excellent places to go and look and listen. Each visit can be a free lesson in collecting, a news broadcast of what hits and misses the upcoming card season may offer.

As the name indicates, the 160-card 1994 Leaf Limited was a limited printing (approximately 300 cases of 20 boxes each). The silver holographic foil masked the game-action backgrounds of each player photo.

39

CHAPTER SEVEN

A DEALER'S CHOICE OF DEALERS

Some call them "card shows." Some call them "sports collectors conventions." Most call them fun. And why not? Baseball card dealers have collections of cards. Card shows have collections of baseball card dealers.

There they are, all under one roof, like a mall full of nothing but hobby shops. Dealers come together for a show, bringing some of their best items. If the first table you stop at doesn't have an Alex Rodriguez card you want, move on. Or if that first dealer wants too much money for the card, see if a seller down the line is willing to listen to offers.

That's right, sometimes you can make a deal. Although show dealers have to pay for their trip to the show, including food, gas (or airplane fare), and maybe an overnight stay in a hotel, many don't have other ongoing expenses. Some card-show dealers do have shops back home. But others just run mail-order businesses. A one-time rental fee for a space at the show is their primary expense. If dealers are spending less money on their business, they might not mind making less profit.

A card show is the place to be for comparing cards and prices. To get the most out of your visit, start by knowing the show. For a smaller event, make sure to call one or two days ahead of time. There's nothing sadder than a family who has traveled for hours to attend an event that's been canceled, the show that never was.

Are the biggest shows the best shows? Not always. The few tables set up at a shopping mall or flea market could have better prices than the sports collectors conventions advertised in hobby magazines.

That's because big show promoters have to pay big appearance fees to persuade current players and Hall of Famers to come and sign autographs. To make that money back, promoters charge dealers big fees for table space and sell admission tickets to collectors. To get more collectors to come, promoters spend more money on advertisements.

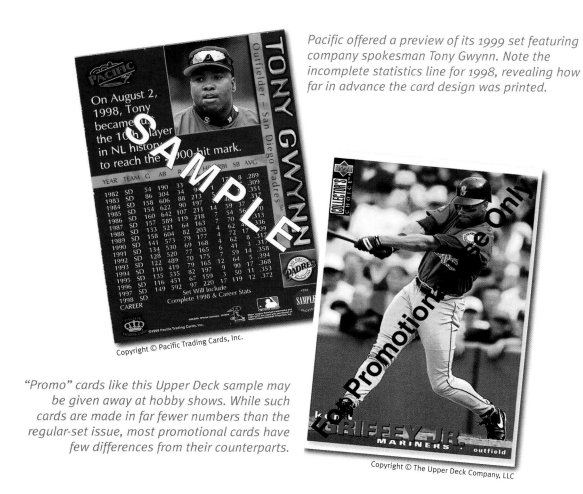

Pacific offered a preview of its 1999 set featuring company spokesman Tony Gwynn. Note the incomplete statistics line for 1998, revealing how far in advance the card design was printed.

"Promo" cards like this Upper Deck sample may be given away at hobby shows. While such cards are made in far fewer numbers than the regular-set issue, most promotional cards have few differences from their counterparts.

Meanwhile, the local show of a few tables could feature "weekend warriors." These dealers are part-timers who have regular, nonhobby jobs. They come to small shows mainly to earn hobby money to build their own collections with, not for food and clothes.

When reading advertisements for larger, regional shows, look at the fine print. Information about corporate sponsors or partners might be listed. If you see the logos for Upper Deck or Fleer or other card-makers in an ad, get excited. Often card companies set up booths at bigger shows. They'll hold contests, have employees answer questions about new cards, or give away the promotional card samples that collectors crave.

A neat promotion that Upper Deck began at shows in the late 1990s was the autograph guest offer. Current and former players would sign an autograph for free, providing the collector turned in a certain number of wrappers from a particular Upper

Deck product. The smartest collectors had read the ads before attending the shows, and brought wrappers with them. You can bet those products were priced at top dollar inside the showroom doors.

No matter what size show a collector wants to attend, it's best to set a game plan first. Here are some shopping strategies that might be helpful:

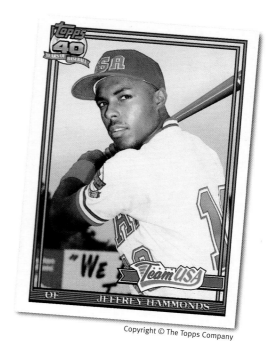

In 1991, Topps' Traded set of 132 cards included that year's top amateurs, members of Team USA.

TIMING YOUR BUY

In the winter fewer people "talk baseball." The sets begin to arrive in December, but when football's Super Bowl is near, it can be tough to get customers talking baseball. Dealers try to use a current-events approach to their inventory. The newest cards from the hottest sport may take up the most table space. Therefore, off-season stuff may offer the best bargains.

This rule doesn't always apply — for example, with value-climbing rookie cards or with cards of big stars like Ken Griffey Jr. Likewise, prices for a team's cards tend to go higher when that team is in a pennant race. What have you got to lose by waiting? Prices often improve at the "wrong" time of the year.

LOCATION MATTERS

If you take in a card show as part of a trip, it's good to do some extra homework. The location of a show can determine not only what you're likely to find but also how much it may cost.

For example, when first baseman John Olerud became a free-agent and signed with the Mariners for the 2000 season, some hobbyists might have thought that this would start his Seattle card sales. But Olerud cards had been selling in Seattle — and selling well — for more than 10 years. Why?

Olerud grew up in the Seattle area. He was a baseball star for the University of Washington. He spent most of his early career with the American League Toronto Blue Jays, who often played in Seattle.

Understanding cases where regional interest pumps up card prices is healthy to hobbyists. Olerud cards in Seattle are more popular — that's why they're higher priced. But hobbyists in southern states might find cards of Olerud or other Mariners to be plentiful — and cheaper too!

EARLY AND LATE DEALS

Hobby history shows that the best deals often happen in the opening, or closing, hours of an event. For instance, if Derek Jeter is signing autographs at your neighborhood card show, expect dealers to want more than the going price-guide value for his cards minutes before he signs. At the end of the day, after the star has left the building, some dealers might discover that all the show attendees brought their own cards for autographs. These leftover cards might now be sold at reduced prices.

Dealers often have two mind-sets. Some may want to make as much money as fast as possible, to pay table rental and travel expenses. Other dealers might be stingy until the final moments of the show. Then, realizing that their sales were disappointing, they'll choose to give you a deal. That way, they'll have *some* money to show for their work — and have a lighter load to carry home.

TIMING YOUR PITCH

Asking a dealer to sell an item for less money might seem harder than, say, homering to straightaway center field in Yankee Stadium. Just remember, anything's possible — though some ground rules can help your odds!

It's best to go one-on-one with a dealer. Time your pitch. Asking the dealer to sell you a two-dollar card for

> "Till this day, I still get a charge out of signing a baseball card of mine. It is definitely a big thrill to be on so many baseball cards. It was my dream to become a major-league baseball player. I think it's a kick to think other individuals would actually want an autograph of mine!"
>
> —Bob Kipper, pitcher 1985 to 1992, on 43 cards. Kipper lost his card collection in a 1997 house fire. Collectors read of his loss, and sent him replacement cards as gifts!

a buck in the middle of a crowd of customers can bring doom. Most dealers will say "No," because they know everyone else listening will chirp, "Hey! Sell to me at half-price too!"

Wait until you're the only one around. Then swing for the fences. (That's baseball talk for "go for it!") Strikeouts happen, but sweetness reigns when the hitter connects. A three-step negotiation may work. Imagine this matchup:

Dealer: That Andruw Jones card books at three bucks.

Kid collector: How about a dollar?

Dealer: I need at least two dollars.

Kid Collector: Sold!

Do the math. See how the card was priced three times, with the price changed by one-third? A price reduction of 25 percent (taking a quarter off for every dollar) is common. A 33 percent reduction (of $3 to $2) is possible. Getting a half-price mark-down can be done, although your chances are like a two-out, bottom-of-the-ninth swing for a grand slam.

If you offer less than half the requested price, you'll probably get a nasty response from the other side of the table. A common dealer response to such "low-ball" offers sounds something like this: "If you think my cards are so worthless, why are you wasting your time and mine?"

Furthermore, don't try saying, "The guy over there sells it cheaper." The likely dealer reply will be, "Fine. Buy it there." Dealers scout their competition. They know their prices have to be at or below other prices in the room. And collectors who try to make dealers oppose each other for lowest prices may get shunned by every seller. Believe it or not, many dealers are friends, and they'll stick together.

From 1975 to 1977, the Washington State Sports Collectors Association produced sets of cards featuring retired stars. The cards helped promote yearly collector conventions in the Seattle area.

PACK YOUR PRICE GUIDE

Do you have a recent price-guide magazine? Be sure to bring it to the next show you attend. It's like having another person beside you to help negotiate your purchase.

These days, most dealers won't bother putting prices on many single cards. Instead, they'll flip open their *Beckett* and tell you how much the magazine estimates those cards are worth. Still, have a magazine of your own. If a dealer is sure the card you want should cost five bucks, instead of the dollar amount the price guide claims, politely point out the difference. It's fine to say, "I was hoping to get the card for book value." Some dealers might agree to meet the price. Others may explain why they want more. Maybe they themselves paid the *Beckett* price, expecting the card to become a hot property in the future. Even if you decide not to buy the card, you'll still get a free education about future hobby trends.

TOOLS FOR SHOPPING

Many dealers seem to see nothing wrong with giving you unbagged, unprotected cards. This endangers the mint condition of cards. So bring your own plastic pages, pockets, binders, and bags. Many dealers will provide them for you, but be prepared for those who don't.

And remember: Dealers have some rightful gripes about customers too. Collectors may go to the commons boxes, pulling cards they're considering out of numerical order. Suddenly, the hobbyist doesn't want to buy all the cards. Not only does the dealer make no money, but he has to ignore other customers while re-sorting and refiling the unwanted cards in their order. Some dealers stop carrying commons because they take so much time and make too little money.

Here's an easy solution for both collector and dealer: Bring a handful of index cards with you. Before you look over commons, show the dealer that you'll mark the places of the cards you want in the box. Say, "I'll keep them in order by number this way. Okay?"

Watch the dealer's face shine. Maybe your thoughtfulness will even get you a better deal for less money.

BURIED TREASURE

Suppose you attend a show in the state of Missouri. All the dealers are selling Cardinals cards they have sorted from their commons piles.

Try asking: "Do you have any regional Cardinals cards?" The dealer might have thought that most people at a St. Louis show would live in the area and already have cards issued nearby. Sometimes, a lack of price-guide information fools dealers into thinking that no one wants the regional cards.

Be patient and specific when shopping at shows. Dealers might have the best and cheapest cards hidden under the table, so that more profitable items can be displayed. Unless you ask the right questions, you may not get the answers you want.

WRITE YOUR WANTS

Surprisingly, few collectors bring a list of their wants to a hobby show. Some shoppers insist they know what they need or like, without writing it down. Others think that the fun of a hobby show is buying the first new cards they see.

These mind-sets may cause a few problems.

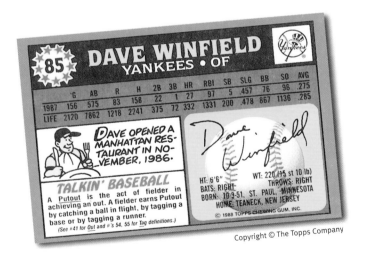

Copyright © The Topps Company

This 1988 American Baseball set of 88 by Topps was designed to be sold in Great Britain. Note the baseball definitions. British measures are used, too, such as weighing players in "stones."

Suppose the box of Bowman's Best packs you opened left you short of a set by just seven cards. Unless you memorize the card numbers you need, you might blow your chance to complete the run of cards for a low price.

Don't be fooled by a big "sale" sign or a fancy table display. Don't bite — or buy! — when a dealer says, "That's the last one. They're selling fast."

Ask yourself: Was this card on your list to begin with? Are you being competitive, trying to buy something just so other collectors won't get it? And is it really so rare? Will the dealer pull three more just like it from under the table once you go?

Most important, your list helps you make a budget. Use hobby magazines and price guides to estimate the going rates of the cards you want. Write down the amount that you are willing and able to spend for each item. Having it in writing will help you tell a dealer, "I wanted that Pacific set, but can't pay more than $15 for it." These steps will help increase your chances of leaving the show with the cards you need — and maybe with a few bucks to spare.

Dealers aren't the only people to speak with at a show. Other customers can help you save both time and money too. If you're at a show with 50 dealer tables, shopping the whole area for the best prices on new Topps packs might take you all day. So if you see someone popping Topps packs in the hotel lobby outside the showroom, ask for advice. "Excuse me, please. Do you remember which dealer you bought those cards from? Could I ask how much they were?" Sometimes, such chats lead to free trading among show attendees.

Even better, you can collect friendships that may last far beyond any card show.

"My favorite card is one that has the National League emblem on the border as a member of the National League All-Star team, showing me in mid-swing. The least favorite is one that looks like a prison mug shot in a White Sox uniform. I obviously wasn't too excited to have my picture taken at that particular time.

"[On the 1985 Topps "Father and Son" card] I was honored to be pictured with my father. At the time, there were not too many father-son combinations to have played major-league baseball. That was special. It gave us a special link to this great game, and I was proud that people would know that I am my father's son."

—Vance Law

47

CHAPTER EIGHT
TRICK PITCHES

Many players call baseball a game of inches. An inch may be the difference between a ball or a strike, a foul ball or a homer. And no matter which way the ball bounces, a good player has to be ready. Baseball card collectors will be safe more often than out by knowing the challenges of this hobby.

AUTOGRAPHS

Suppose you read that your favorite New York Mets player will sign autographs at a huge hobby show. The price for in-person signatures is $25.

Maybe you think you'll save some bucks by just writing to him in care of the team for a free autograph. You've got a Fleer Ultra that'll look great signed. Then your card will be worth $25 more. Right?

Time out! Don't bet on any of the above coming true. Just because a show promoter charges $25 for an in-person autograph doesn't prove the value of the signature. The promoter has to pay the player for time and travel, and make his own profit too. Another promoter could offer the same signer next month for $5. That price doesn't prove the autograph's value, either.

Mailing for autographs has its problems too. First of all, the player you like may sign by mail, or he may not. He may sign for free, or he may not.

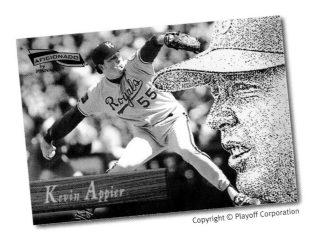

Copyright © Playoff Corporation

Pinnacle's 1996 Aficionado set of 200 cards might be the oddest issue of the decade. Woodgrain panels for names etched in gold were offset by sepia-tone photos and a holographic rainbow foil portrait.

Suppose this Met in question does. That's still no reason to send your best, most expensive card to him for a signature. Current major leaguers get more fan mail than ever before. Teams try to get all the mail sorted and delivered, but there's no guarantee that a Met written to "in care of Shea Stadium" will get every single letter. And even if he does, your card could get mashed and trashed in transit, making mint condition a foggy memory. The safest route is to send only less-valued duplicates in the mail, in case they don't succeed in their search for a real signature.

Which brings up another point: When (and if) your card gets returned, is it really autographed? Some players are overwhelmed by fan mail. They use a rubber stamp or an autopen machine to copy their signatures. The real autograph may look like the copy, but that doesn't mean the actual player ever came close to your card with a pen. The result is a card in poor-to-fair condition, no better than if your little brother laced your card front with spray paint. Hobby purists insist that even an authentic autograph on a card destroys mint condition.

Topps' 1990 Heads Up set of 24 players was designed with a suction cup and strip of tape on each card back. Trouble was, collectors didn't rush to hang floating baseball heads on walls.

In other words, you'll never know if an autograph has lasting cash value. It will to some people, it won't to others. The only reason to get an autograph is if it means something to you, if you want to feel a little closer to the athlete you admire. Standing in line for an in-person signature may or may not get you that closeness. Sure, you'll see his face and hands better than you could from the stands. You might get to say hello or ask a quick question. But chances are just as great — especially if the player is a star facing a huge crowd — that you'll be rushed through so that others can get a turn too. The player may be so busy signing that he'll barely look up at your face. You may be left with nothing but a card with an inky scribble on it.

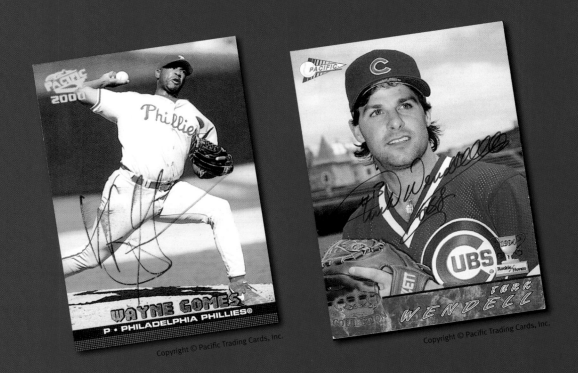

From the 1994 Crown Collection to Pacific 2000, players are anxious to sign cards they like.

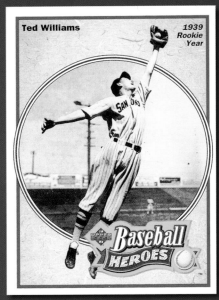

When companies first began including inserts like these Upper Deck Baseball Heroes, wrappers didn't tell collectors their odds of finding a special card. These 10 Williams inserts were in selected 1992 packs.

THE CARD THAT NEVER WAS

Sooner or later, someone will offer you a card and say, "No one has ever seen a card like this!" But even if your best friend believes this card is for real, it never hurts to check it out.

The first things collectors fear from such "one-of-a-kind" cards is that they're counterfeit. That is, they look like they're from a well-known company, but they were really printed somewhere else. But counterfeit cards are harder to make than phantom cards. That's why phantom cards are a much bigger problem.

Phantom cards are not licensed by Major League Baseball or the Players Association. Phantoms might picture a player on a college or high-school team. Perhaps only a simple black-and-white photo graces the cards. Such cards are often made by someone who got a photo or an old picture and decided to print off some cards, thinking anything with a star's face will sell.

The shady seller might claim that the card was only available in one city or that it was a "warehouse find." This popular myth tells how the printer ran out of money and couldn't ship the cards to dealers. Years later, this lucky dealer found these undiscovered cards collecting dust. At least, that's how the story goes.

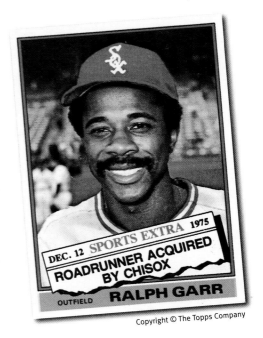

Copyright © The Topps Company

This 1976 example shows how Topps once painted over photos to update cards when a player was traded.

One clue to an illegally made card is if the back is blank. Only one side of the card was printed, to get the bogus product out on the street as soon as possible. And no copyright (the little © in a circle) is listed.

If a card is not in any price guide, if it's never been written up in a hobby magazine, think twice. Phantom cards aren't worth your money.

THE EMPEROR'S NEW CLOTHES

Another trickster is the repackager. Visit most department stores, and you're sure to find glitzy card packages. The box may be a collection of unopened packs or maybe a grouping of singles.

Suppose you see a promised number of inserts will come in the repackaged package. You see at least one superstar's face. Don't get fooled by a vague term like "insert." Some inserts will appear in every pack! Is that so special?

Additionally, some repackagers advertise "Out-of-Print Cards" or "Five-Year Assortment." But the age of a card doesn't necessarily mean value. Collectors don't start paying sky-high prices as soon as a card turns one year old!

Another popular line on repackaging is "Price guide value exceeds $100!" or something similar. This could be true. However, what price guide did the company use? More important, what year was that price guide published? As you know, not all cards go up — or stay up — in value.

Counterfeiters used an unusual ploy when reprinting the 1975 Topps' "rookie" card of Hall of Famer George Brett. They marked their work as a "reprint." But the card back also featured blotchy printing, a clue that the work might not be genuine.

Topps sent free cards to military members serving outside the country during the Persian Gulf War against Iraq in 1991. Overprinted with a special gold-leaf insignia, nearly 6,800 sets were produced.

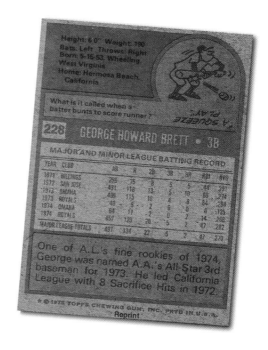

RICKEY HENDERSON

A card like this Rickey Henderson may never be listed in any price guide. Why? It was not licensed or approved at the time by Major League Baseball or the Players Association. The card back contains no marking or clue as to the maker.

WHO LET THEM IN?

It's unlikely that a dealer will chase you down the street, begging and bullying you to buy a card set. But some dealers invade a collector's own home!

Numerous TV shopping networks have appeared on the screens of unsuspecting collectors, using baseball stars to help sell their deals.

Shoppers can be blinded by baseball stars who sit with a sales host. Between words, the athlete nods and smiles at the next card item for sale. Sure enough, the huge price flashing on the screen is reduced! A lower price has been offered. Interestingly, however, the TV price often towers above any price-guide figure.

To sweeten the sales pitch, buyers who call might get the chance to speak to the baseball great.

If you do watch a collectibles segment on a TV shopping network, keep a price-guide magazine at hand. Promise yourself that you won't ask an adult to call in a purchase just because you like the athlete co-host. Listen to the claims and see how much the brief thrill of a possible telephone chat with a celebrity might cost. Even with the card delivered to your home, chances are the TV prices could be triple the going hobby-shop rates. With the extra money you do not spend on overpriced collectibles, you might be able to buy a ticket or two to a real game.

"Players were contacted by an agent representing the baseball card companies. The fee in those days was either gifts or money. The companies usually gave you a few boxes of the cards. Very few players saved the cards in the late 1940s and 50s. My children played with the cards."

—Pete Castiglione, pictured in four Bowman issues and the 1952 Topps set

SPENDING ON VENDING

It's not an evil robot, but the steel box almost calls to you. Amid the machines selling candy bars and drinks, a few outlets have related devices selling packs of cards.

The problem here is simple. Have you ever been peeved when a vending machine drops your chocolate cream-filled snack from the top shelf, squishing it before you can catch it? Why should those cards come out of the machine any more gently? Mint-condition cards have never been squeezed and folded between metal prongs. High dives off vending-machine shelves make for ugly card corners.

Think of collecting as if it were a baseball game. Many, if not most, players love the game, respect the rules, and play fair. Likewise, most card sellers and buyers are fans first, people who love baseball and collect cards as a way to stay close to the game. Don't think that every collector and dealer you meet in the baseball-card hobby is out to trick you. Most just want to play the game.

Playing means making decisions. Take the pitch or swing? Different choices bring different rewards, or problems. Knowing — and preparing for — problems before they happen is the best way to keep a winning hobby game plan.

CHAPTER NINE
YOUR HOBBY GAME PLAN

How are you managing your hobby? In baseball, a good manager makes good game plans. For the good of the team, to keep the team winning, the manager will make substitutions and other changes.

As a collector, you need to have the same talent. Can you make changes if your money starts to disappear or you're getting bored with one type of card?

Here are some game plans that can help any collector:

REDEFINE YOUR COLLECTION

You're a baseball card collector. Why should that mean you collect only piles of cardboard rectangles? Think of all the sidelines you could find to help showcase the set you're collecting.

Most important is the wrapper or package the cards come in. In the 1990s some hobbyists went wild trying to find surviving wrappers for cards from the 1960s through 1980s. After all, most collectors threw away the packages after they got what was inside.

Another reason wrappers are rare is that companies used to want wrappers returned. Companies still have mail-in offers that promise special card sets or other collectibles, as long as wrappers are mailed in as proof of your product purchase. Collectors who go to the trouble of answering mail-in offers are

Donruss made this 26-card tribute set to Nolan Ryan available only in 12-packs of Coke products, one card per pack.

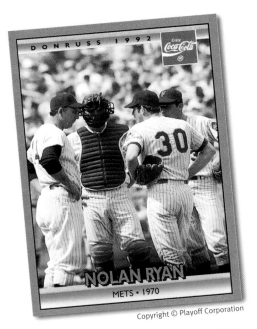

Copyright © Playoff Corporation

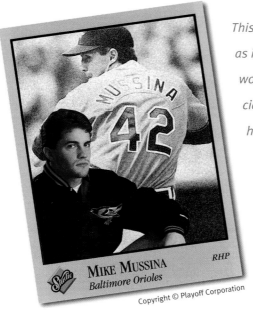

This 1992 Leaf set's name was simple: Studio. Players posed, as in a studio. Card backs were even more fun. Each player would offer personal information, such as his favorite musician, author, movie, best friend in baseball, or the person he'd most like to meet.

getting true collectibles. In future years, those wrapper redemption prizes may be more valuable than any of the cards found in the packs.

Next, check at card shops for what you don't see. Is the dealer throwing out empty boxes that housed baseball packs? Did the dealer get posters or shelf displays from the company to advertise the set? Are those display items being used? What will happen to them when the dealer is done with them? Ask about items you might be interested in adding to your own collection. Anything made by the manufacturer of the cards you're collecting should be considered for your collection, especially if the price is right. And free is a very good price!

DON'T LAUGH AT KID STUFF

Have you asked a police officer if he or she has any cards? Some law-enforcement agencies have printed "safety" sets of major-league, minor-league, or college players. Cards have ideas printed on the backs about how to stay safe and smart, warning against drugs, gangs, and other dangers.

From 1984 through 1991, artist T. S. O'Connell made his own cards. Over the years, O'Connell created 250 different cards, printing just 2,000 of each.

Cards have been made by other groups too — to get kids to read more, to study more subjects, even to attend church. Religious groups sometimes print cards with inspirational messages about a player's faith.

Try talking to your teachers, librarians, or youth-group leaders. They may know of groups that are making such cards.

In all of these cases, the cards are designed with kids in mind. But even if you don't keep the cards in your own collection, they'll still make good trading material. Adults are often too shy to ask for the cards, or fail in getting them from other adults. Adults can only dream of being given cards to collect, free of charge! Sometimes, it's good to be young.

SHOP EVERYWHERE

Go to the grocery store and look carefully — at *everything*. Dog food. Meat. Cheese. Cereal. Frozen pizza. Candy bars.

These are only a few products that have offered cards to increase sales. The cards may be inside the package, or you may have to mail in labels. Read carefully! Many offers want your cash-register receipt too, so be sure not to throw that away.

"But I don't have a dog," you may say. Or, "Mom won't let us eat candy bars."

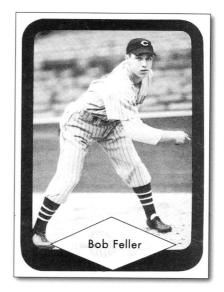

Into the 1970s, card sets would be made by show promoters to celebrate hobby conventions. This 1975 issue of 24 cards in Des Moines, Iowa, was titled "Great Plains Greats" from the Great Plains Sports Collectors Association.

A five-card set was available at the Dodger Stadium in 1999 to kids only, free for the asking at souvenir stands.

In 1990 the Dodgers created an 1,100-card set. The sheets of cards were given out at selected home games. The set tried to depict every member of every Dodgers team from the franchise's first 100 years.

Maybe your grandma's dog would eat the food. Or the dogs at the local animal shelter. Maybe your best friend would like the candy. It might even be something his mom buys regularly, and she'd be happy to save the wrapper for you.

So tell people about your hobby! They may be able — and happy — to help.

THERE'S NO PLACE LIKE HOME

Not all Yankees collectors live in New York.

Those devoted hobbyists might shrug when their state university team is featured on a card set, maybe at a fast-food place that gives away a few new cards each week.

"Those aren't the Yankees," such collectors might grumble.

Not yet.

Never forget tomorrow's stars as you're choosing today's cards. Who can say those college players will never become Yankees? The cards you ignore may not be available in 49 of the 50 states. Talk about cornering the market! Regional cards are available only during the season, for shorter times than national issues. Get regionals while you can, at least as extras to sell or trade.

EXPECT THE UNEXPECTED

How soon do you give up as a collector? If you discover that a team like the Chicago Cubs passed out a card set during one game, do you think that only fans who attended that game (or dealers with connections) will have those cards?

Hopeful hobbyists often find the biggest bargains. If a team has a giveaway, it's worth the price of two stamps to write and ask if any cards remain. Of course, enclose a self-addressed, stamped envelope for a reply.

Try to discover the name of a front-office employee of your favorite team (online is a good place to look), so your letter won't be answered at random.

Make your request short and sweet. Here's a sample:

The 1954 Johnston Cookies set featured 35 members of the Milwaukee Braves. Cards measured only 2 by $3\frac{7}{8}$ inches.

CHARLES GORIN

Dear (team name, or team employee):
   I am (number) years old. I've been a fan of the (team name) for (number) years. I always listen to games on radio and TV, and follow the team in the newspaper. I've collected cards for many years too.

   I'd love to have the cards that were given away at the (date) game. I'm sorry I missed attending. If any cards remain, could I learn how to obtain one set of the cards for my collection?

   Thank you.
   Sincerely,
   (your name)

One of the keys to success is to be personal. And before writing, make sure you're not older than the maximum giveaway age. (Some teams will advertise a bonus as being "for all fans age 14 and under.")

Now consider another hobby possibility. What if you read in a hobby newspaper about an Atlanta Braves set sponsored by restaurants in Georgia. Do you have to hop a bus to locate the cards?

Try the Internet, or find a librarian who can get you a reference book listing company addresses. Find the headquarters of the company (not the team) that is sponsoring any regional set.

Make your letter something like this:

Dear (fill in company sponsor name):
I am a (number)-year-old fan of the (team name) and was happy to learn your company has sponsored a set of their cards.

I'm sorry that none of your businesses are close to where I live. I have no way to be part of your promotion. Is there any way I could obtain a set of the cards for my personal collection?

Thank you.
Sincerely,
(your name)

1947 ROOKIE OF THE YEAR

JACKIE ROBINSON

Dodger season-ticketholders in 1997 were rewarded with a six-card set honoring some of the team's past rookies of the year.

Suppose that a place like a Pizza Hut or Safeway grocery store sponsors the cards. Maybe there's the same franchise in your town, but this store isn't part of the regional card giveaway. Be creative. See if you can talk to the manager of your local franchise. Explain that you are a regular customer and that you'd like help getting the baseball cards. If you've seen magazine pictures of the card, bring a photocopy. Maybe that manager is friends with the manager of a store in the area giving cards away.

If not, try sending a cash-register slip or product wrapper to the headquarters when you write for more information. You should offer proof that you support that business. Most of all, describe your shopping and eating habits. Does your whole family like the

Card-maker Michael Aronstein's Sports Star Publishing Company issued a 630-card set of current players in 1976. Keith Olbermann, now a famed sportscaster for ESPN, wrote some card backs. In 1981, Aronstein's renamed company, TCMA, produced a set called The 1960s, creating 189 cards of the biggest (and smallest) names from that decade.

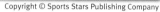

burgers or groceries that the card-sponsoring company sells? Add one sentence that tells how old you are and how many in your family use those products. Companies know that kids are now choosing the foods and products they'll buy for years to come. Even if you aren't a big spender now, companies hope you'll choose their brands in the future. Maybe sending you some free cards will help you make up your mind, no matter where you live.

LOVE ALL LEAGUES

Atlantic League. Frontier League. Northern League. Western League. They have little to do with Major League Baseball.

That's why you should consider collecting these cards.

Independent teams are dotted with former major leaguers wanting one more shot at the bigs, along with hopefuls who could come from nowhere and be next year's headlines. In 1998 the St. Paul Saints gave away a set to kids during one game. Within a year, dealers were getting as much as $50 for the 32 cards. Why? J. D. Drew, who would be a St. Louis Cardinals starter in a year, highlighted the set from Minnesota. Reportedly, only 4,500 sets were made.

The possibilities for baseball buried treasure don't end here. Keep your eyes, ears, and mind open, ready to get in the collecting game. Think fast and think of the future.

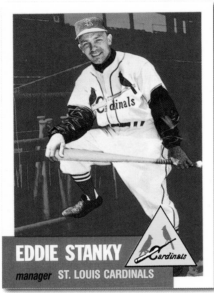

Copyright © The Topps Company

Topps' original 1953 set featured color paintings of players. When Topps reprinted the set in 1991, it added more than 50 cards of 1950s players not included the first time. Topps called the "new" black-and-white photo cards "The Cards That Never Were."

Card sets often feature subsets filled with young players, the players of the future. But what will cards of the future be like? What will card collectors have to look forward to — or look out for — in the 21st century?

For starters, cards and teams may work together like never before. At the beginning of the 2000 season, cards and protective sheets were given out to all kids at selected games in all big-league cities. These sheets contained two hard-to-get cards from a 32-card set of cards made by the four major companies together: Upper Deck, Topps, Pacific, and Fleer/SkyBox. Because all four companies helped create the set, mailing in wrappers from any of their products would help complete the set.

Major League Baseball and the Players Association both want cards to sell well. Companies pay millions of dollars yearly in licensing fees to these two organizations, to get permission to use team names and logos, and to use the names and pictures of individual players. In the past, the Players Association put aside some money made from card companies for emergency pay during strikes (when paychecks stop).

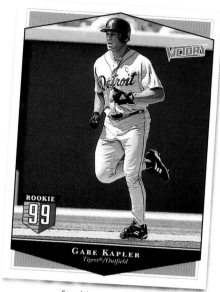

Both organizations get to approve which companies get licenses to make "official cards." But the card companies can decide to stop making cards altogether, if there isn't enough profit.

COMING ATTRACTIONS

In the future, expect cards to be used to earn prizes. Show your cards at a hobby shop or ballpark and get team clothing or other souvenirs. It may be like earning tickets from playing arcade games, then exchanging those tickets for prizes. Except in this case, collectors will insist on getting their cards back along with the prizes.

Yesterday's cards may return for a finale. Topps gave collectors a second chance at "unaffordable" sets from 1952 to 1954 with their reprinted Archives series. In 1983, Topps began by reprinting the 1952 set. The reprint was available only by mail as a complete set for $40. Not many people responded. Fifteen years later, the few remaining reprint sets sold for $300 and up.

Tomorrow's cards may consist of any material. No longer will collectors believe that

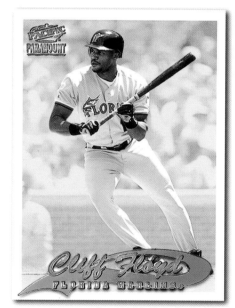

The 1999 Pacific Paramount set of 250 cards could be found in six parallel versions. The big difference was the color of the foil on card fronts.

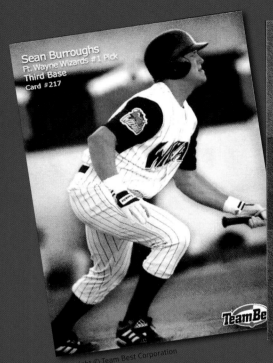

Sean Burroughs
Ft. Wayne Wizards #1 Pick
Third Base
Card #217

2000 ROOKIES OF

PAT BURRELL

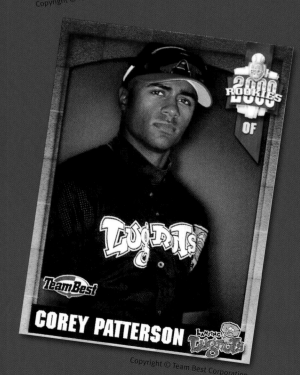

2000 ROOKIES OF

COREY PATTERSON

Don't think that every card from one set will look the same. In the 2000 Rookies set by minor-league card-maker Team Best, only some cards of first-round draft picks have gold borders. The airplane logo is for Babbitt's Bombers, an insert series of the top sluggers in the minors. The inserts are named for photographer Ken Babbitt. Only one in 72 packs might produce a "Bomber."

"card" is just an abbreviation for "cardboard." In the 1990s, inserts were produced on leather, canvas, and metal. In the future, who knows?

All of this won't be free. Teams and players will still get paid something to be on cards, and companies will want their profit too.

How much profit? Older collectors were shocked in 1989 when Upper Deck was the first company to ask more than $1 per package! No one will ever pay it, claimed the veteran hobbyists. Yet less than a decade later, few blinked at the five-card packs of Fleer's "Sports Illustrated Greats of the Game." One pack cost $15. The only promise was that one autograph came per pack. No one knew which autograph, or how plentiful that signature would be. Still, card-makers found that, if enough collectors were tempted, price was not an object.

WHICH GOOD OLD DAYS?

Don't be surprised if some older collectors are gloomy about the future of the hobby. They may say they'd like to see several card companies fail, go out of business altogether. Why?

Many collectors don't want so many choices. They may claim that with the glut of new sets there's no way to collect everything. If only one company made cards again, everything would cost less, they say.

These people have very selective memories about the "good old days."

Prices of Topps cards did rise more slowly in the 1960s and 1970s, but it

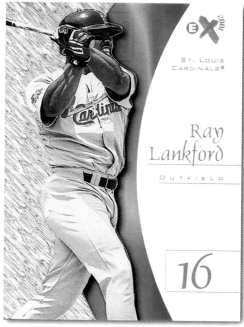

Copyright © Fleer Trading Cards

Etched holofoil on 20-point plastic made Skybox's 100-card E-X2001 set seem like stained-glass artwork.

Comic book art inspired the 1997 Fleer Metal Universe set. At the time, Marvel Comics was owned by Fleer.

wasn't until Topps faced competition from Upper Deck, Score, Fleer, and Donruss in 1989 that Topps made major improvements in its cards. To keep up with the competition, Topps started including color photos on card backs, using glossier white stock and making a better variety of sets.

And think about this: If only one source remained for baseball cards, couldn't that company charge any price it wanted? Likewise, would that surviving company have any reason to take risks in creating unusual sets and other new ideas?

Not all veteran collectors see a gloomy future for the hobby. Some who have been active since the 1950s have seen so many hobby changes that they feel ready for any surprises. Frank Barning, author of *Sports Collectors Digest's* "Barnstorming" column about card collectors with unusual goals, has such an open mind.

"There is a good chance that [in the future] many of the card manufacturers will sell directly to the public, thus cutting out the cost of the middlemen, wholesalers and dealers. Such sales will be via the Internet," Barning predicted.

"Collecting will continue to make dramatic changes," he went on. "The major tool of change [will be] the Internet. A decade from now, practically everyone in North America will be

Let's get small! These Donruss cards measured just $1\frac{1}{4}$ by $1\frac{3}{4}$ inches. The 72 shrunken wonders were prizes, one per Cracker Jack box.

Beginning in the 1970s, assorted companies began reprinting sets by long-gone card-makers. Older collectors protested at first, afraid that affordable reproductions would ruin values of the real things. Other hobbyists worried that reprinted cards could be aged and altered to pass for the actual cards from years ago.

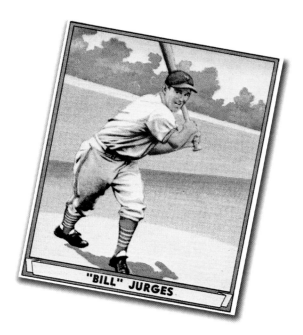

online, and auction services such as eBay will have replaced many of the card stores and shows."

Barning continued: "It is expensive for a card dealer to own a store and/or take his collectibles on the road to sell at card shows. Online auctions have very little overhead for sellers, so that is where much more of the action will be.

"I signed my first contract with Bowman Gum in 1950 for $150. Most of my [card] pictures were taken in New York [at] the Polo Grounds, Ebbets Field, Shea Stadium, and finally Yankee Stadium. All photos were in May and June."

—Bob Friend, pitcher, 1951 to 1966

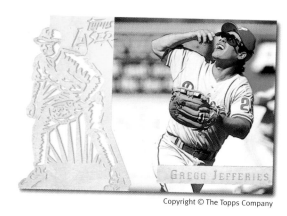

*Every one of the 128 Topps' Laser Cut cards
from 1996 featured some detailed trimwork.*

"At the same time, buying online will be the place of choice for collectors. Instead of driving to a card show and paying admission, [shopping] online is easier —and there is no admission charge."

Barning believed that in the 21st century, "the amount of cards and other collectibles online will dwarf what is available at stores and shows, even major ones. Plus it will be much easier to comparison shop for bargains online as the Internet technology for searching is improved. In the future," Barning concluded, "the buyer will be the king, not the dealer."

No matter what products card companies may launch, collectors can certainly be winners. The hobby will vote with its purchases. Each dollar you spend tells dealers and companies what cards matter most to you, the collector. Spend wisely, and be heard.

*Upper Deck's 1990 set contained unusual,
fun photos on both fronts and backs.*

"I really wasn't aware of cards of players as collector items when I was a boy. Baseball cards were good to put in the spokes of my bike and made a great noise as I rode the streets. I never dreamed that they might be of value. They only accompanied Topps bubble gum, and we weren't allowed to have much of that. It was bad for the teeth."

– Vance Law

APPENDIX

Unlike players in the 162-game baseball season, card collectors can enjoy the sport any day of the year. If you yearn to learn more about the hobby, try these sources first:

Sports Collectors Digest, 700 East State Street, Iola, WI 54990
www.sportscollectorsdigest.com

This weekly is like a huge newspaper, with more than 200 oversize pages. Being published so often means that readers might get a new set's checklist at least two weeks before a monthly magazine can release the news. SCD is known most for tons of advertising. The ads range from mail-order dealers to specialized collectors who buy classifieds for help completing little-known, almost-done sets.

Beckett Baseball Card Monthly, 15850 Dallas Parkway, Dallas, TX 75248
www.beckett.com

This monthly magazine was the first in the hobby to focus solely on baseball cards. The publisher began with a baseball card magazine, then branched out with new titles for other sports cards.

The magazine is in full-color, except for the famed price-guide center section. The price guide offers the best listings of different insert cards that appear in packs yearly.

Don't miss "By the Box." This section offers data about opening all the packs in a box from a new card product. Was the box enough to complete a set? Did the reported odds of insert distribution match what the packs in the box offered? Even if everyone's luck is different, seeing someone else's findings from opening so many packs helps others decide if the purchase is worthwhile.

The monthly "Card Gallery" is another famed section in the magazine. Here's a chance to see one of every card from the hardest-to-get inserts. Most collectors may never see one of these inserts, let alone a photo of the whole set!

Unlike SCD, expect most Beckett articles to focus on the newest cards and current stars.

GLOSSARY

album: 1. a three-ringed binder, to display cards kept in plastic sheets; 2. a paperback book for displaying collectible stickers.

assortment: a grouping of cards. The term implies that every card in the group is different. But there may be more than one of some cards unless the grouping has a label such as "100 *different*."

autograph: 1. a card signed by the player shown; 2. a signed card of that player, autographed in limited quantity, certified as a real autograph by the manufacturer, then inserted in random packs.

Beckett: a registered trademark of Beckett Publications. The name of price-guide founder Dr. James Beckett is used often as a guideline for the value of a card. If a dealer will sell at "half Beckett," that means the card would cost half of the price listed in *Beckett Baseball Card Monthly* magazine.

blankback: a normal card, except that all the printing was omitted from the back. Often, a blankback was a printing mistake. Many collectors see blankbacks as incomplete cards with lesser value. See also *wrongback*.

blister pack: a see-through, cardboard-back package. Some cards are visible through the plastic fronts of blister packs.

book: short for "book value," as from a price-guide book (or magazine).

border: a framelike stripe surrounding the photo area on the front of a card. For a card to be mint, all borders must be equal.

box: a vending container issued by card companies to be used by retailers. Usually containing 24 to 36 packs, a box may contain a certain bonus card, sometimes printed on the box bottom, as a reward for buying all the packs.

boxed set: cards sold in a complete set by the company. Often, boxed sets may be as few as 33 cards, containing only stars or rookies. Some boxed sets may be offered through only one store.

card stock: the paper or cardboard used to print the card. Card stock is judged by its thickness and color.

case: a sealed carton offered by a card company, containing a specified number of factory-collated sets or boxes of card packs.

cello: (SELL-o) 1. an assortment of cards with wrapping that allows a buyer to see at least one card available in an assortment of cards; 2. an older hobby term, referring to see-through cellophane wrapping.

centered: relating to a card's image placed properly in the middle of the card. A card with an off-center photo is not considered mint.

checklist: 1. a complete listing of every card in a set; 2. a card that lists part of the cards in a set. Only unmarked checklists are considered "mint."

collate: to put cards from a set in numerical order.

collectible: 1. a card or cards worthy of a collector's attention; 2. noncard items of memorabilia; 3. something worth money.

collector: someone wanting to have baseball cards for fun and later, perhaps, for profit.

combination card (or "combo"): a card featuring more than one player. Often, each of the players will be noted by name on the card front. Photos showing game action involving more than one player are *not* combination cards.

commemorative: a card made to highlight one event, such as Mark McGwire breaking the home-run record for a season.

common: one of the least-wanted cards in a set. The player depicted is not popular or in demand, making the card affordable and easy to get.

condition: the look and shape of a card.

convention: a large gathering of card dealers and collectors who buy, sell, and trade cards. A convention may last for several days, and is open to the public. Smaller gatherings are called "card shows."

convention issue: one or more cards produced to promote a sports collectibles show. Often, the cards are only available at that show. Conventions issues are sometimes sold, sometimes given away.

correction: a card issued by a manufacturer to correct an error on that card. The latter version may be more or less collectible, depending on its availability.

counterfeit: an illegally reprinted version of a card, which has no value but is wrongly sold as the actual card.

crease: a bend or fold that harms a card.

dealer: a person who buys, sells, or trades cards to make a profit. The dealer may also collect, but making money is the first goal.

decollate: to place cards in random order to be inserted into packages, a task often done by machine.

die-cut: a card with part of its stock cut out, often to create fancy shapes.

display: retail items, such as posters or other advertisements, used in stores to help sell baseball cards.

double-printed: relating to a card that was issued in twice the quantity as other cards. When the company printed the sheet of cards, that card appeared one time more than the others.

duplicate (or "dupe"): a duplicate is the exact same card as another.

error: a card with incorrect statistics, information, or photos on its front or back. Many errors go unfixed by the card companies, which may limit those card values.

extra: see *duplicate*.

factory-collated: relating to a complete set, sorted by the manufacturer and sold as a unit.

first card: the first time a player appears in a set, such as Topps. Not to be confused with rookie card.

food issue: a card or set made to help promote or sell certain food products.

franchise: a company that places stores or restaurants by the same name in many towns. Burger King is one example.

grade: to judge the condition of a card, looking at its creases, bent corners, and other possible problems.

graded: relating to a card that has had its condition judged by a professional grading service. Services assign a score to the card, depending on its condition, such as 10.0 for a perfect card.

Hall of Famer: a player who has been elected to the Baseball Hall of Fame in Cooperstown, New York. His cards may rise in value.

hand-sorted: relating to a complete set of cards assembled by hand from numerous individual packages.

high numbers: the last series of a card set to be issued in packs. In the past, the last series was produced in lesser quantities and was harder to find.

hobby only: relating to cards available only through hobby shops and card dealers.

hologram: 1. any of a number of specialized foil-like stickers and cards that give an image or photograph a three-dimensional appearance; 2. Upper Deck's diamond-shaped company trademark, placed on card backs to discourage counterfeiting.

hot pack: a pack in which every card is an insert or specialty card.

insert: 1. a card printed in limited quantities and randomly placed only in selected packs. Not considered part of a regular card set; 2. a noncard item, such as a poster or sticker, inserted one per pack to increase sales.

international issue: a card or set available in more than one country, not always published in English. May feature major league players.

issue: 1. to make available; 2. one set or card from a single source, such as a "Fleer issue."

laser-cut: relating to cards designed and cut into unique shapes, often with pieces removed, all done by a laser.

lenticular: relating to cards using a special hologram-like technology to make photos seem alive and three-dimensional.

limited edition: an overused and misused term hinting that cards from that set will be in short supply. In the past, companies would not tell if the edition was "limited" to thousands — or *millions*!

lot: an assortment of cards, related in some way, such as the same player, team, or set. The cards are sold as one unit.

mail-in cards: cards that could only be obtained from the company by mail. Often, mail-in cards require money and empty card wrappers.

manufacturer: a company that creates a product. For example, Topps is a manufacturer of cards.

memorabilia: noncard items such as autographs, team publications, and equipment. See *collectible*.

miscut: a card improperly removed from the printing sheet. The card will have uneven centering and may be oddly shaped.

misprint: a card affected by poor printing, with a blurry photo, ink blot, or other untidy look.

multi-player card: see *combination card*.

multi-sport: a set featuring cards of players from baseball and other sports.

National: short for National Sports Collectors Convention. This yearly event is one of the nation's largest card shows and is held at a different location each year.

odds: the chances of finding an insert card in a pack. Also called *ratio*.

off-center: relating to a card with uneven borders.

Olympics card: a card showing specific baseball players in Olympic competition.

panel: two or more individual cards attached, sometimes by a perforation.

parallel card: a card that is almost a twin of a regular card from a set, except for a special touch, such as embossed or die-cut features.

perforation: a dotted line, slightly cut, to show where cards can be separated or removed from a sheet. Dividing cards along perforated lines lessens their condition.

plastic sheet: plastic or vinyl sheets with pockets to display and protect cards.

premium: 1. a special card or prize offered by mail from a company; 2. cards with more expensive special features, such as a thicker stock.

price guide: a book or magazine listing suggested cash values for cards. Prices rise and fall with time, so the date that a price guide was issued is important.

promo: one or more cards used to promote a company, event, or future card set. Usually, promos are free samples or gifts for people attending a collectors convention.

prototype: an early design for a card, which may differ from the future set. Sometimes, these cards are given as samples.

random: only in some packs.

rare: an overused, often misused hobby term hinting that a card is the hardest to find, harder to find than "scarce" cards.

redemption card: a card that, when mailed in, can be redeemed for special cards or prizes.

regional: relating to cards distributed only in certain geographical regions. Regional card sets may focus on one team and be circulated only in the area near the team.

reprint: a later printing of an old card, clearly marked as a "reprint." Some reprints come in a smaller size or different card stock to avoid confusion with originals.

retail only: relating to cards available only through non-hobby stores, such as K-Mart or Wal-Mart.

reverse: 1. the back of a card, showing statistics or biography; 2. a photo that has been printed backward because its negative is turned wrong-side-up during printing. Uniform numbers or writing will appear backward, or a right-handed player will look left-handed in a photo reverse.

rookie card: a beginning player's first appearance on a regular card in a nationally issued set from a major company. A rookie card can be either the player's first regular card or his draft-pick card during his first pro season — but not both. If a player doesn't appear in a certain set until years after his career begins, that card will *not* be considered a rookie card.

safety set (also known as a police set): a set of cards whose backs have positive messages about obeying laws and behaving well. Sometimes the cards are given away to kids one per week by police officers.

SASE: self-addressed, stamped envelope, sent to help get a reply by mail.

scarce: see *rare*.

second-year card: the second card of a player in a major nationally issued set. This card may be the first time the player appears without other rookies.

series: a portion of cards in a set. For instance, a 400-card set may be issued in two stages, offering the first 200 cards in the first series.

set: a collection containing one of each card from one basic set, not including insert cards. The set of 1999 Upper Deck cards contains 525 cards, numbered 1 through 525.

short-print: a card made in lesser quantities than others in the same set.

skip-numbered: not numbered in perfect sequence. Some card numbers may not exist, because a player was left out of the set following injury or contractual problems.

sleeve: a card-size plastic pouch used to protect and display one card.

standard-size card: $2\frac{1}{2}$ by $3\frac{1}{2}$ inches

subset: a group of cards within a regular set, such as seven cards honoring the World Series.

team issue: cards created and distributed by the team represented on the cards.

team set: a collection of all cards depicting members of one team from one set. Once offered only by dealers who would sort cards into teams and resell them in groups. Some companies now sell the assortments themselves.

three-dimensional: relating to cards with photographs that seem to move when tilted. Some three-dimensional cards may have images of more than one player.

tin: a decorative metal container or lid sold as a package containing one card or set.

uncut sheet: a sheet containing more than one card, left uncut by the manufacturer.

unlicensed: relating to a card or cards made by companies that didn't pay a licensing fee to Major League Baseball, meaning that photos cannot contain team logos.

variation: a slightly different version of a card. Variations usually occur when the company sees a mistake on a card and tries to fix it. "Variation" can refer to either the error card or the corrected card.

wax pack: an individually wrapped pack of cards. Previously, cards came in wrappers made of waxed paper.

wrongback: a card with the back of another card from that set. A wrongback is more common than a blankback, but neither may have increased value.

BOOKS

To collect your own baseball-card information, start by thinking about a hobby library. Numerous worthwhile books are available from Beckett Publications, with new editions published regularly. Krause Publications, which issues *Sports Collectors Digest*, also has a huge line of hobby-related books.

Both Krause and Beckett create worthy encyclopedia-like books that retell the history of many cards and checklist whole sets, including regionals. Another helpful book, with versions created by each publisher, is an alphabetical checklist. For example, to find out how many cards Kirby Puckett appeared on during his career, you no longer have to read a decade's worth of checklists. Why study lists of more than 600 cards to find only one name? Instead, look up "Puckett, Kirby," and find his card's numbers from any year he was featured.

Once, collectors had to depend solely on hobby publishers to purchase such books. Now, online booksellers abound, offering books at discounted prices. Places like www.amazon.com give customers room to post reviews of good and bad books they've purchased.

Of course, most books about baseball cards will focus on price-guide values. But that's a risky business, hoping that a book quoting any card's value will be accurate a year later. Most collectors prefer monthly or weekly updates, or even daily briefings on card values from the Internet. The yearly price-guide books seem best for collectors wanting a complete listing of every card from every set ever made. That's a service magazines don't have the time or space to provide.

One book is vital for anyone serious about getting autographed cards by mail. *The Baseball Address List* is published every two years by Jack Smalling. He is the autograph-collecting pioneer who started uncovering home addresses of current and former players, coaches, and even umpires.

Teams often lose track of former players. Smalling's book is the next best thing. However, since 20 percent of Americans move each year, an outdated address cannot be avoided sometimes. Still, at no extra charge, Smalling will send updated addresses to his readers when they send their old "Return to Sender" envelope front, and a self-addressed, stamped envelope for his reply.

Smalling even sells monthly updates of his book in the form of computerized printouts, promising the latest addresses of players who have moved. Contact Smalling at 2308 Van Buren, Ames, IA 50010.

Writing to players in care of teams (with self-addressed, stamped envelopes) is another possibility. However, don't send a card you would hate to lose. No teams or players make promises they can or will return every card safe and signed.

ADDRESSES

Major League Baseball
350 Park Ave., New York, NY 10022
www.majorleaguebaseball.com

American League
350 Park Ave., New York, NY 10022

Anaheim Angels
2000 Gene Autry Way
Anaheim, CA 92806
www.angelsbaseball.com

Baltimore Orioles,
333 W. Camden St.
Baltimore, MD 21201
www.theorioles.com

Boston Red Sox
Fenway Park
Boston, MA 02215
www.redsox.com

Chicago White Sox
333 W. 35th St.
Chicago, IL 60616
www.chisox.com

Cleveland Indians
2401 Ontario St.
Cleveland, OH 44115
www.indians.com

Detroit Tigers
Comercia Park
2100 Woodward
Detroit, MI 48201
www.detroittigers.com

Kansas City Royals
P.O. Box 419969
Kansas City, MO 64141-6969
www.kcroyals.com

Minnesota Twins
501 Chicago Ave. South
Minneapolis, MN 55415
www.mntwins.com

New York Yankees
Yankee Stadium
Bronx, NY 10451
www.yankees.com

Oakland Athletics
Oakland Coliseum
Oakland, CA 94621
www.oaklandathletics.com

Seattle Mariners
P.O. Box 4100
Seattle, WA 98104
www.mariners.org

Tampa Bay Devil Rays
One Stadium Drive
St. Petersburg, FL 33705
www.devilray.com

Texas Rangers
P.O. Box 90111
Arlington, TX 76004
www.texasrangers.com

Toronto Blue Jays
SkyDome
1 Blue Jays Way, Suite 3200
Toronto, Ontario, Canada M5V 1J1
www.bluejays.ca

National League
350 Park Ave., New York, NY 10022

Arizona Diamondbacks
P.O. Box 2095
Phoenix, AZ 85001
www.azdiamondbacks.com

Atlanta Braves
P.O. Box 4064
Atlanta, GA 30302
www.atlantabraves.com

Chicago Cubs
1060 W. Addison St.
Chicago, IL 60613
www.cubs.com

Cincinnati Reds
100 Cinergy Field
Cincinnati, OH 45202
www.cincinnatireds.com

Colorado Rockies
Coors Field
2001 Blake St., Denver, CO 80205
www.coloradorockies.com

Florida Marlins
2267 N.W. 199th St.
Miami, FL 33056
www.flamarlins.com

Houston Astros
P.O. Box 288
Houston, TX 77001-0288
www.astros.com

Los Angeles Dodgers
1000 Elysian Park Ave.
Los Angeles, CA 90012
Web site: www.dodgers.com

Milwaukee Brewers
P.O. Box 3099
Milwaukee, WI 53201-3099
www.milwaukeebrewers.com

Montreal Expos
P.O. Box 500, Station M
Montreal, Quebec, Canada H1V 3P2
www.montrealexpos.com

New York Mets
Shea Stadium
Flushing, NY 11368
www.mets.com

Philadelphia Phillies
P.O. Box 7575
Philadelphia, PA 19101
www.phillies.com

Pittsburgh Pirates
Three Rivers Stadium
Pittsburgh, PA 15212
www.pirateball.com

St. Louis Cardinals
250 Stadium Plaza
St. Louis, MO 63102
www.stlcardinals.com

San Diego Padres
P.O. Box 2000
San Diego, CA 92112
www.padres.org

San Francisco Giants
Pacific Ball Park
24 Willie Mays Plaza
San Francisco, CA 94107
www.sfgiants.com

OTHER ADDRESSES

**National Baseball Hall of
Fame and Museum**
P.O. Box 590, Cooperstown, NY 13326
www.baseballhalloffame.org

Fleer/Skybox International
Executive Plaza
1120 Route 73, Suite 300,
Mount Laurel, NJ 08054
www.fleer.com

Pacific Trading Cards
18424 Highway 99
Lynnwood, WA 98037
www.pacifictradingcards.com

Team Best Corporation
7115 Oak Ridge Pkwy., Suite 180
Austell, GA 30168
www.teambest.com

Topps Trading Cards
One Whitehall St.
New York, NY 10004
www.topps.com

Upper Deck
5909 Sea Otter Place
Carlsbad, CA 92008
www.upperdeck.com

For the ultimate address aid, consider *Baseball America's Directory: The Complete Pocket Baseball Guide*. Since the 1980s, this paperback has offered front-office directories for all major- and minor-league teams. It's possible to learn the name of a specific team employee. You can write for information about past or present card sets.

To get the book, which is updated yearly, contact Baseball America, P.O. Box 2089, Durham, NC 27702, or go to www.baseballamerica.com.

New sources in print and online appear regularly. Ask dealers and librarians to suggest the best new information outlets. And, when you find good hobby news, share it with others who collect.